Guarding
Alaska

Captain Jeffrey Hartman USCG (ret)

iUniverse, Inc.
Bloomington

Guarding Alaska
A Memoir of Coast Guard Missions on the Last Frontier

iUniverse books may be ordered through booksellers or by contacting:

iUniverse
1663 Liberty Drive
Bloomington, IN 47403
www.iuniverse.com
1-800-Authors (1-800-288-4677)

Because of the dynamic nature of the Internet, any web addresses or links contained in this book may have changed since publication and may no longer be valid. The views expressed in this work are solely those of the author and do not necessarily reflect the views of the publisher, and the publisher hereby disclaims any responsibility for them.

Any people depicted in stock imagery provided by Thinkstock are models, and such images are being used for illustrative purposes only.

Certain stock imagery © Thinkstock.

ISBN: 978-1-4759-2479-4 (sc)
ISBN: 978-1-4759-2478-7 (hc)
ISBN: 978-1-4759-2477-0 (e)

Library of Congress Control Number: 2012908414

Printed in the United States of America

iUniverse rev. date: 7/10/2012

To the Kala Point writing group: Chris, Summer, David, Carol, and Leslie for their encouragement and to Sara, Sylvia, Nicole and Lynn for their support, suggestions and proofing.

Contents

CHAPTER TWO

Figures

Preface

Guarding Alaska

Coast Guard Missions on the Last Frontier

This is about Alaska and what the Coast Guard does there. It's a personal memoir of my experience in Alaska both as witness and principal. I was a career Coast Guard pilot and officer; we at times seem to have a language of our own. In this book there will be technical terms, and jargon, which I will explain in the text. I will also include a glossary for reference. For simplicity I will use the military 24-hour clock to denote time, which starts at midnight and continues for 24 hours. Thus 1 P.M. is 1300. I also use the term "Service" to represent "Coast Guard" at times.

Herein are my experiences, education and stories to define what the Coast Guard does, or rather did when I served my thirty-year career. I will use Alaska to showcase these missions and the missions to showcase Alaska. What the Coast Guard does in other locations is important; but doing it in Alaska often makes it more complicated. The opinions expressed are my own and do not reflect official Coast Guard policy.

Introduction

Two of my favorite things, the Coast Guard and Alaska, are what this book is about because both are often only partially understood. I hope *Guarding Alaska* will correct that.

Alaska For the First Time

Alaska goes by a number of names. "The Great Land", or in the Aleut language Alyeska, The Last Frontier, are all used interchangeably with Alaska. Seeing Alaska for the first time I understood fully why it is called "The Great Land," and it took my breath away. I was assigned to the aviation detachment on the USCG icebreaker *Northwind,* and we were sailing Gastineau Channel toward Juneau for our first liberty port. I stood on the flight deck mesmerized by what I was seeing all around me. It was June 1967 and mountains on either side of the channel were gorgeous with green lush vegetation, thousands of wild flowers, and dozens of waterfalls. The air was crisp and clean with the smell of salt water and evergreens. Then we docked.

Once we moored the reality of civilization set in. Between the Coast Guard dock and the Governor's Mansion on the hill were unsightly rusty corrugated metal dwellings that resembled a supersized tin can cut in half. These were Quonset huts, a temporary shelter left over from World War II (WW II), but still in use. This was Alaska, a dichotomy. It has unbelievable natural beauty too often marred by man's trashing. I was a lieutenant junior grade (LTJG) at the time, four years out of the US Coast Guard Academy. My aviator wings on my uniform were a year and a half old having earned them in the Navy Training Command in Pensacola in December 1965. In the parlance of the Service, I was a nugget.

The Coast Guard's history in Alaska is also mixed. It includes some of the greatest rescues of all times. It also has one of the largest maritime pollution disasters in this country in a pristine, environmentally sensitive place, in which the Coast Guard was officially partly to blame. On a bizarre note the Coast Guard is responsible for the introduction of reindeer into Alaska.

Guarding Alaska

Guarding Alaska is also about Alaska's history, geography, dangers, delights and the Coast Guard's part in it as I learned and lived it during four Coast Guard tours of active duty there. These tours of duty included:

- Aviation Detachment on five-month deployment to the Arctic in 1967 flying helicopters from the icebreaker *Northwind*.
- Flying helicopter rescue missions out of Kodiak Island 1974,75.
- Chief of Search and Rescue for the Coast Guard in Alaska from July 1982 to June 1984.
- Chief of Readiness July 1988 to January 1993 when I was responsible for contingency planning and managing a program called Maritime Defense Zone (MARDEZ), Alaska, which is very similar to what has become Homeland Security.

Following my 30-year Coast Guard career, I spent four years with the Alaska Department of Natural Resources as Assistant Director of Administrative Services, and later as Special Assistant to the Commissioner where I learned even more about the good, bad, and ugly of Alaska. The ugly includes Alaska politics where a tiny population, approximately half that of San Antonio Texas, has a state budget of $8.4 billion. It's a very expensive place to do anything including govern. I was a part of, or witness to, most of the stories here. The early Revenue Cutter history and the Service's experiences in WW II were before my time, however I studied extensively about both. Some of it I learned during my Masters program in Public Administration at the University of Alaska Southeast. I've found Alaska, and the Coast Guard's part in it fascinating.

Chapter One

Alaska Took My Breath Away

Dimensions, Diamonds, Dangers & Defining
Dimensions

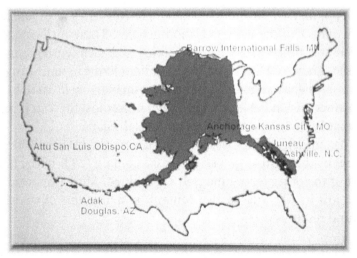

Map of Alaska superimposed on that of the contiguous 48 states

Once when I was briefing congressional staffers who were on a visit to Alaska, I used a slide similar to graphic 1-1 depicting Alaska superimposed on a map of the lower 48. The staffers laughed as they said Senator Stevens used the same illustration frequently in trying to impress his colleagues. Despite the humor, the point was that getting around in Alaska is difficult. Even with its vast distances, there are less than 5,000 miles of paved roads.[1]

Land

The land area of Alaska is 570,374 square miles. The population according to the Alaska Department of Labor and Workforce Development was 710,231 in 2010. Of this population, 291,826, or nearly 42%, were in Anchorage.[2] It's said in Alaska (outside Anchorage) that the good thing about Anchorage is that it's close to Alaska, meaning it has all the big city problems not common in the rest of the state. The second largest city is Fairbanks at 31,627 followed closely by Juneau, the capital at 31,275. Sitka is the fourth largest with 8,881. Rounding out the top five is Ketchikan at 7,728.[3]

People

The population includes 106,000 Natives (17%), or as the Canadians call them, First Nation peoples. These include eight different ethnic groups living in fairly well defined regions of Alaska. They are Tlingit and Haida Indians living in southeastern Alaska, Athabascan in the interior, Tsimshian living in Metlakatla on Annette Island, Aleut in the Aleutian Islands, the Yup'ik and Inupiat Eskimos and the Alutiq on Kodiak Island. [4]

A common joke in Alaska is that if it were divided in half, Texas would be the third largest state. Alaska contains 20% of the land area of the other forty-nine states combined. More importantly than just its size, Alaska also contains vast amounts of valuable natural resources.

---

1   The Alaska Almanac, 32nd Edition, 88-9

2   *Alaska Economic Trends*, September 2011, 13

3   ibid

4   The Alaska Almanac 32nd Edition, 154-5

Diamonds

Alaska really doesn't have diamonds, or at least they haven't been discovered yet, but it has nearly everything else of value, and in great abundance. The natural resources include gold, silver, copper, molybdenum, zinc, coal, timber, fish, crab and of course oil and gas. The mineral value of its production of the top four, lead, silver, gold and zinc for 2009 was $2.3 billion.[5] It also has some of the worst weather, least developed infrastructure, at least half of the U.S. earthquakes, most annoying mosquitoes, and the most dangerous animals outside Africa. But there are no snakes.

Location, Location, Location

Alaska's location at the top of the world makes it strategically important as both a transportation hub and as a rapid response base to go anywhere on the globe. Ted Stevens International Airport in Anchorage was the busiest airport in the US for air cargo landed weight in 2006.[6] This is typical of the dichotomy of Alaska - the state with the second lowest population and fewest paved roads has one of the busiest airports for freight. From Alaska it is quicker to fly to both Europe and Asia than it is from the continental United States.

Natural Resources

Oil and Gas

Alaska is rich with resources. Within its borders is the Trans-Alaska Pipeline (TAPS) and oil platforms in Cook Inlet that provides 17% of the nations' oil supply.[7] The North Slope, which is well known for its oil, has an even greater abundance of natural gas. The proven gas reserve of this area is thirty-seven trillion cubic feet.[8] Natural gas is a clean alternative to coal for electricity generation. This is critically important to Japan, which buys a large percentage of the world's liquefied natural gas. When Alaska

---

5   Alaska Economic Trends, September 2011, 9

6   The Alaska Almanac, 32nd Edition, 63

7   ibid, 167

8   The Alaska Almanac, 32nd Edition, 167

develops the means to get the gas to market, the national economy will be significantly improved. Environmentally, natural gas is a better choice as heating homes since natural gas and not coal reduces pollution and improves the environment for us all.

Fresh Water

Even more importantly for the arid future, 40% of the fresh water of the United States is in Alaska.[9] Approximately three quarters of the fresh water is contained in the state's rapidly melting 100,000 glaciers and ice fields.[10]

Food From the Sea

The ocean waters of Alaska contain vast quantities of renewable protein if properly managed. Alaska fisheries account for 53% of the U. S. fish landed in 2010 with a total of 4.3 billion pounds.[11] In a day when the nation is concerned with its trade deficit, it's worthy of note that Alaska's biggest customers are the far eastern nations. The potential markets are even greater if the resources are appropriately managed. As the Coast Guard is charged with the safe operation of the nation's ports and waterways, all of this is of concern to the Service.

Dangers
Bears

The threat for death from bear attacks is greatly exaggerated. A study done by the Alaska State epidemiologist showed that bear attacks killed only twenty people in the first eighty-five years of the 20th century.[12] The state does have an abundance of bears, however, and those who venture into the wild are cautioned to be aware.

9 Food Safety & Sanitation Program, *Bottling Alaska's Water,* (Anchorage, Alaska Department of Environmental Conservation, 2011) 1

10 The Alaska Almanac, 32nd Edition, 82

11 Alaska Economic Trends, November 2011, 3

12 "Tips You Should Know When Entering Bear Country", (*Alaska Outdoor Journal.* 1996), 1

There are four types of bears in Alaska, black, brown, glacier (blue) and polar (white). Brown bear numbers are estimated to be 40,000, with black bears being much more common at 100,000.[13] Kodiak bears are included in the Ursus Arctos classification just as are the brown bear, which are known as grizzly bears.

Polar bear numbers in Alaska are hard to come by, however the U. S. Fish & Wildlife Service estimates the worldwide population at 22,000-25,000 in nineteen different populations in Alaska, Canada, Greenland, Norway, and Russia.[14] It is generally accepted that they are dwindling with the loss of ice habitat. In May of 2008 the U.S. Fish. & Wildlife published a final rule that the polar bear was a threatened species. The somewhat rare glacier or blue bear is sub-specie of black bears normally found in the Southeast region. I've never seen a Blue bear in the wild but there is a wonderful one mounted on display at the Juneau airport.

When I reported in to Kodiak Air Station in January of 1974, my sponsor was Lieutenant Commander Jack Denninger, class of '62. Jack was a pilot's pilot and earned two Distinguished Flying Crosses during his operational flying. The day we checked in, Jack and his wife Pat had stocked our refrigerator, made our beds and had a crab casserole on the stove. He also gave me two books saying, "Read these, and pass them along when you are a sponsor!" The two books were *The Thousand-Mile War* by Brian Garfield, and *The Monarch of Dead Man's Bay* by Roger Caras. The first book was about WW II in the Aleutians, and the second was a fictional account of a giant brown bear. It was a wonderful book in that it gave many insights into the habits of brown bears and their environments. My entire family has enjoyed it over the years.

---

13   "Alaska Bears", *Alaska Trekker*, (Anchorage, 2011), 1

14   *Marine Mammals Management*, (U.S. Fish & Wildlife Service, Alaska Region, 1 November 2011), 1

Bear tracks with Corgi

During my time in Alaska I had many bear experiences. Most came when I was flying a helicopter and were good for some interesting pictures although not particularly exciting. A half dozen came when I was in the woods or mountains hunting deer, Rocky Mountain goats or Dall sheep. Being eye to eye with a bear on its terrain is definitely exciting. The closest I came to being one of the statistics was with my hunting partner, Mike Stenger.

A Bear Story
The Hunt

We were returning to the crest of Crown Mountain on Kodiak where we had left a mountain goat that Mike had shot a few days earlier. After dressing out the goat Mike and I and a third partner, Stan Bork had pitched our two tents. Mike and I were sleeping in a two-man pup tent he had sewn himself because he didn't trust production equipment. Stan, and all our gear, was in a second tent we had checked out from the Kodiak Support Center's morale locker. The morale locker carried recreational equipment that could be rented or in some cases loaned out. It was usually not top-of-the-line equipment.

The Weather Factor
Weather forecasting back in those days before satellites was somewhat hit or miss. This night was definitely a "miss." We noted darkening skies and hurried through our dinner and turned in before the rains started. That night Alaska demonstrated that she was not for the unwary.

A serious Alaskan storm blew up with high winds and horizontal rain. The tent rainfly was useless as the heavy rain blew in under it, and we were soon soaked in our sleeping bags. Suddenly Stan appeared out of the shrieking wind and rain filled black night and climbed in with Mike and I in the two-man tent. "Didn't you guys hear me yelling for help?" he angrily shouted. He was soaked and not particularly happy that we had not joined him in saving our gear.

He told us that the winds had buckled the aluminum poles in the morale tent and had completely blown it down and rolled it several yards with Stan inside. Stan had covered it with rocks the best he could to keep things from blowing away even more and then retreated to us. Needless to say we spent a miserable, cold and wet night.

Running For Our Lives
I remember thinking that if the wind increased only ten knots more we would be blown away. I also remember praying "God, if you get me out of this, I'll never go hunting again." The next morning we were all approaching hypothermia and knew we had to get down to where we could build a fire to dry out and get warm. The three of us packed up what was left of our camp and covered the goat with rocks intending to return when the weather abated. We safely made it back down to sea level where we pitched camp and huddled around a fire for two days until our contracted pilot picked us up.

The younger author on ridge leading into Crown
Mountain basin on Kodiak Island

Back For More

Mike and I agreed that we should attempt to retrieve his goat meat
from the mountain, in that state hunting laws made it unlawful to
waste game meat. We again contracted with our pilot to fly us in,
this time to be in and back in one day. Our plan was to climb up
the 3,000 foot plus mountain and back with the goat in the same
day. Each of us only carried a handgun, Mike had a 22, and I had
borrowed a 357. We took basic survival rations and light packs
for the flight in by floatplane. All went well until we reached the
basin with the alpine lake where the goat was buried. Rounding
a large boulder we came face to face with a small (300 pound)
brown bear finishing up the last of Mike's goat. In all the bear
books I had read, one of the situations to be absolutely avoided
is surprising a bear with its food. It is second in danger only to
surprising a sow with cubs.

Stenger said, "If he charges, jump in the lake." I thought it
was probably a lousy option as the bear was likely a much better
swimmer than either of us. We were lucky however in that the
bear smelled us and didn't like it and took off for the high country.

We did make it back down in time but ended up with about five pounds of usable goat meat. As they say in the commercials, " but memories – priceless."

Alaskan Weather

The weather in Alaska can be dangerous and often is. Forecasting in the 1970's when I was flying helicopters from Kodiak was more art than science. High winds are common, made even more unpredictable by the high terrain along the coastline of most of mainland Alaska and the Aleutian Islands. High winds also mean heavy seas. Waves of fifty feet can occur.[15] These often result in maritime disasters, which mean helicopter rescues. Heavy snow and icing were common in the six months of coldest weather from October through March. January in Kodiak has an average temperature of 29.9 degrees F and precipitation of 9.5 inches.[16] Reduced visibility due to fog is common year round.

A classmate of mine, and brother aviator, Denis Bluett, told me a story when he was flying the old Grumman fixed wing amphibian aircraft, the UF2G. This aircraft was officially called the Albatross but affectionately known as the Goat. He was a new pilot at the air station and as a joke the instructor had him start the aircraft in the lee of the hanger during a high wind. Once he started taxiing and came out from behind the hanger, the wind caught the tail and caused the big aircraft to end for end and start sliding on the ice. It was only by expert use of the throttles by the more experienced pilot that the aircraft was brought under control.

During my tour at Kodiak as head of the Training Department, we started the Kodiak Survival School. This school was intended to teach survival basics for a crew that was stranded in a coastal maritime environment. Prior to this we had been using the USAF cold weather school, at Eielson Air Force Base near Fairbanks, which was intended for survival in an inland situation. While this was a valuable experience, it was not the environment that

---

15   ibid, p, 47

16   ibid, p. 49

the Coast Guard pilots normally operated in. We were more likely to be forced down in a coastal setting. We would need to know how to make a shelter out of driftwood rather than snow. Also gathering of food is entirely different. I participated in one of the first classes and was fortunate to catch my dinner, a snowshoe hare, with a snare that I had set. It was one of my proudest trophies and it was as enjoyable as any gourmet meal after 24 hours with no food.

Daylight

The amount of daylight is a fact of life in Alaska and a factor in attempting rescues. Night vision goggles were not available when I was flying and searching for an object such as a disabled fishing boat with no power for lights was daunting in the dark. In Juneau in Southeast Alaska, at winter solstice in December, there was only a little over six hours of daylight.[17] On a less dramatic note, the lack of daylight means that for much of the winter you go to work and come home in the dark. This can be depressing for some.

Chief of Readiness

During my final tour of duty in Alaska I was Chief of Readiness and Reserve. This was a catchall position that covered military and contingency planning, small arms training, running the district armory where the small arms were stored and relations with other military organizations. A bizarre example from my first Readiness tour in Boston was that when the admiral was invited to march in a parade with his staff I was responsible for refreshing everyone on the sword manual of arms. This included such things as "present swords," "order swords" and so on. We practiced several days so that when we actually marched in the parade we could perform the sword movements properly.

Part of the Alaska readiness job involved planning, running and evaluating mobilization exercises for reserve personnel assigned. Whenever we would host Navy and Coast Guard Reservists from "outside" (a term that Alaskans use to refer to anyplace but Alaska)

---

17   ibid, p. 58

for military exercises, the first thing we had to impress on them was how life-threatening Alaska weather could be.

The author with a dinner on survival training on Kodiak

Earthquakes
Earthquake Mechanics

Earthquakes result when the gigantic "plates" that form the surface of the earth move relative to each other. Where these plates contact each other a fault line results. In the devastating Good Friday quake, as it later became known, the Pacific plate slid beneath the North American plate 80 miles north of Anchorage and twelve miles underground.[18] What resulted was an 8.6 magnitude quake on the Richter scale. Other accounts, including the 32nd edition of *The Alaska Almanac* list the earthquake's magnitude at 9.2.

According to seismologists a quake of this magnitude would result in the following: few masonry structures would be left standing, bridges would be destroyed, broad fissures would form in the ground, underground pipes would rupture, and railroad rails would be bent greatly.[19] I would add to this somewhat stale description the sheer terror of having your entire world thrashing about you and nothing whatsoever you could do. If this destruction were not enough, it is magnified when an earthquake occurs under the ocean or near the shoreline. It produces a terrifying sea wave, known as a tsunami, which can travel thousands of miles. Unfortunately Alaska is earthquake prone and has more coastline than any other part of the U.S.

Stan Cohen in his excellent pictorial history, *8.6, The Great Alaska Earthquake*, gives the following statistics. Alaska has 11% of the World's earthquakes and has 52% of all the earthquakes in the United States. Seven of the ten largest earthquakes ever recorded in the United States were in Alaska. On average, Alaska has a magnitude eight or larger earthquake every thirteen years and ninety magnitude four or five earthquakes per year. The 32nd edition of *The Alaska Almanac* said that in February 2004 the Alaska Earthquake Advisory Center located 2,964 earthquakes in or near Alaska.

Tsunamis
The mechanics of generating the killer waves called tsunamis are not well understood, and for maritime nations, such as Japan, they are deadly. The waves travel great distances and at great speeds. In the open ocean waves can reach speeds of up to 600 miles per hour.[20] Their tremendous destructive power becomes evident as this huge amount of energy reaches coastal waters and

18   Cohen, *Earthquake*, 2

19   *Operation Helping Hand*, v

20   Cohen, *Earthquake*, iix

the velocity is traded for wave height. Often a withdrawing of the water from the coastal area heralds the wave's approach. It is a serious warning because following it are giant waves that have been known to crest as high as 100 feet.

Good Friday Earthquake 1964

I saw first hand the damage to coastal communities in South-central Alaska and Kodiak Island caused by the 1964 quake and tsunamis everywhere I looked. Two hundred and fifty miles south of Anchorage, the Island of Kodiak was changed forever. Eleven years later when my family was stationed on Kodiak we could still see the aftermath, including a large steel ship which had been pushed so far inland that it was left where it was and made into a locally popular nightclub called the Beachcomber.

The nightclub Beachcomber ashore at Kodiak

Kodiak Island Damage

The town of Kodiak was built on bedrock so the initial ground movement caused little structural damage. That night, however, the town was destroyed, by a series of ten seismic sea waves that hit the area, as was most of the fishing industry and fleet. Thankfully, the town's people had received word that the tsunami waves were coming and had climbed to higher ground on Pillar Mountain behind the town. Kodiak suffered massive destruction to its businesses and to its homes. The waves, reaching a maximum height of thirty feet, destroyed 108 homes, forty-five fishing boats, eight industrial and forty-five commercial structures. It also left over 600 people homeless, or nearly one-quarter of the town's population at the time.[21]

A fellow Coast Guard officer, Ron Potter, was being transferred, and he and his wife had all of their personal effects packed up in a warehouse awaiting shipment. They never saw their possessions again as the tsunami waves dispersed it all over Old Woman's Bay.

Kodiak waterfront following tsunami wave

The critical breakwater was destroyed and even the nourishing mud at the bottom of the harbor had been sucked out, so that the anchors of the remaining boats afloat could not get a grip on the now rock bottom. The earthquake sank the town and the harbor floor an amazing five feet. The seismic forces caused large areas of the earths' surface to rise and others to sink.

21   *Operation Helping Hand*, 42

Anchorage Damage
The devastation to Anchorage is well known and was even displayed on the 10 April 1964 cover of *Life* magazine. Many buildings were destroyed. The control tower at the Anchorage International Airport collapsed killing one of its controllers. The entire south side of Fourth Street had to be cleared of destroyed buildings for several blocks.[22]

4th Avenue Anchorage following 1964 Good Friday earthquake

Five people lost their lives in the Anchorage area including one man who tried to move his parked car only to have a portion of the five story J. C. Penney building fall on it, killing him. The Office of Emergency Planning estimated the total damage to Alaska to be over half a billion in 1964 dollars, with 60% of that loss sustained by Anchorage.[23] While the Anchorage devastation was well known, the loss of life and permanent damage to other coastal communities was proportionally even greater but not as well known outside the state.

---

22   Cohen, *Earthquake,* 2

23   ibid

Valdez Impact

Valdez is now the southern terminus of the giant Trans-Alaska Pipeline. It was made infamous by the *Exxon Valdez* oil spill, in a bizarre coincidence, on the 25th anniversary of the great quake. Valdez was so badly destroyed by the earthquake and subsequent gigantic submarine earth slide that it was decided to abandon the historic town site and rebuild four miles to the west.

The price in human loss in this small community was tragic with thirty-seven people losing their lives. The local jaw dropping tsunami wave was recorded to have snapped off two-foot diameter spruce trees up to 1000 feet above mean low water in the area.[24]

Whittier Impact

Whittier is a small railroad port on the east side of Prince William Sound built during WWII to provide a year round terminal for the Alaska Railroad for bringing in supplies from sea. Of the seventy persons living at Whittier at the time, thirteen disappeared with only one body recovered. The earthquake destroyed a major portion of the port facilities. In fact, with the loss of the port facilities in Whittier, Seward, and Valdez there were no all-weather port facilities in operation to handle cargo for Anchorage and Fairbanks, the two most populated cities in Alaska.[25]

---

24   ibid, 30-4

25   ibid, 36

Seward 1964 tsunami damage. Note wooden posts driven
through concrete by the force of the earthquake

Seward Impact

Seventy-five miles south of Anchorage, Seward was one of the
most heavily damaged Alaskan cities. Located at the head of
Resurrection Bay the city is surrounded by mountains. At the
time of the quake, Seward's economy depended on the port as
well as the movement of cargo and fuel from the large Texaco and
Standard Oil tank farms by the waterfront. These facilities were
completely destroyed by a combination of underwater landslides,
locally generated waves, fires, and the tsunami wave.

The ground movement at Seward was so violent that people
were totally unable to stand without holding on to something.
Perhaps the most unique effect of the quake was the offshore

ground sliding that caused layer after layer of the waterfront to break off and slide into the bay. In some areas up to a 500-foot wide area of waterfront property disappeared into the bay. [26]

USCG Air Station Kodiak Impact
The Coast Guard Air Detachment was a tenant of the Kodiak Naval Base eight miles from downtown Kodiak. The base suffered serious damage when the tsunamis flooded the hangers to a depth of several feet. Fortunately, the aircraft had either been flown away or towed to higher ground prior to the waves arrival.

Part of the long-term damage at Kodiak, and elsewhere as well, resulted from the fact that the ground actually sank nearly six feet due to a phenomenon known as tectonic subsidence. The result was that at high tides many of the structures were actually flooded. One of the piers on Old Woman's Bay is awash at high tide because of the quake. This became known as marginal pier and was used to store buoys and anchor chain while I was stationed there. It was of no consequence if they were immersed at the occasional higher-than-normal tide.

Coast Guard Air Station Kodiak 1990

26   ibid, 44-5

The aircraft stationed at Kodiak at the time had been moved to higher ground and were available for rescues after the disaster. However the main hanger was flooded to a depth of several feet and the repair shops suffered extensive water damage. The Navy was the landlord of the Kodiak base at the time of the quake. They proved a good neighbor to the civilian residents of Kodiak that had had their homes demolished by the disaster, as the galley served 12,000 meals to the evacuees in the first forty-eight hours.[27]

My wife Sylvia, holding six-month old Brad and 3-year old Nicole on Jewel Beach in Kodiak 1974

One unusual occurrence that resulted in a boon for the children to be stationed with their parents on Kodiak was the appearance of Jewel Beach. This was a great favorite of the children stationed on Kodiak. Because of the lowering of the ground level, the previous landfill was now under water. Over the years the bottles, and pieces of discarded ceramic and glass

27   *Operation Helping Hand*, 43

items became broken and polished by the tidal action and sand. The result was that these glass "jewels" would wash up on the black sand beach for the children to find and collect. My family kept several coffee cans full of these "jewels" thirty-seven years later.

Personal Observations on the Earthquake

My classmates and Academy roommate, Ray Heller and Denis Bluett saw the powerful effects of the quake on Alaska up close and personal. The ship they were serving on was the *USCGC Minnetonka* (WPG-67) a sister ship to the *Pontchartrain* that I was assigned to. Both the *"Ponch"* and the *"Minnie"* were home ported at Pier Charlie in Long Beach harbor. In March of 1964 the *Minnie* was underway in Alaskan waters on a fisheries patrol. Back in those days, before enactment of the Fisheries Conservation and Management Act, or 200-mile limit, there wasn't much that could be done to control foreign fishing vessels that stayed outside our three-mile territorial waters. These were primarily Russian and Japanese trawlers. The *Minnie* was carrying a Department of Fish and Wildlife enforcement officer who kept track of the types and amounts of fish caught for fisheries management background. On the night of 27 March the *Minnie* was patrolling south of the Alaskan peninsula, and Ray was on watch as the Underway Officer of the Deck (OOD).

What was a quiet watch was shattered when the radios on the bridge began erupting with many calls for assistance resulting from the tsunamis generated from the earthquake. One of the closest distress calls came from the fishing vessel *Blue Ocean* that had been washed into shallow waters and had been pushed over on its side. The *Minnie* proceeded to the distressed ship's location and stood by during the night until a small boat could be sent in at first light to evacuate the *Blue Ocean* crew. The district commander in Juneau next ordered the *Minnie* to proceed west to Unimak Pass to prepare to evacuate the Coast Guard crews of the remote and isolated Cape Sarichef and Scotch Cap lights if it became necessary. These two lights marking the Pacific entrance and Bering Sea entrance to Unimak Pass had been the first two Alaskan coastal lighthouses constructed. Scotch Cap light had been built in 1903, with Sarichef following a year later. After all this, I should say that of the nearly fourteen years my family and I spent in Alaska, we never experienced a serious earthquake.

Chapter Two

Peeling the Alaska Onion

Early History

There are certain periods and historic events that have defined Alaska. Some of them included the Coast Guard or its predecessor, the Revenue Cutter Service. These events are what make modern Alaska the unique and captivating state it is. At the heart of the Alaska onion I will peel are the early people. It is generally postulated that the earliest inhabitants most likely traveled across a land bridge from Siberia over 20,000 years ago. In the ensuing next 15,000 years or so they gradually inhabited the Central area, the Southeast area, the Bering Sea coast and the Aleutian Islands.[1]

Russian Period (1741-1867)

The next historical peel was the Russian period. During the last half of the eighteenth century the Russians exploited Alaska. They decimated the otter populations in the Aleutians and enslaved the native population to do so. Permanent Russian settlements were established at Unalaska, Kodiak and Sitka. The Russian Orthodox Church sent missionaries, and the Russian Orthodox Churches were established in many locations.[2] The Russian Orthodox Church in Kenai is one of the oldest buildings in Alaska. A favorite

---

1   Gates, *The Alaska Almanac, 32nd Edition*, 95

2   ibid, 95

summer event at Kodiak was the presenting of the play "The Cry of the Wild Ram," which chronicled the life of Alexander Baranof who was the head of the Russian colony there and the Russian Governor. The play was a major event in Kodiak's small fishing town and involved as many as 400 locals in its production.

Alaska's Purchase (1867)

At the urging of Secretary of the Interior Seward, President Andrew Johnson approved the purchase of Alaska from Russia for the critically advantageous price of $7.2 million. Looking back it was genius; at the time however, many thought Seward was a fool and the purchase became known as Seward's Folly. The treaty was signed 30 March 1867 and the transfer took place on 18 October 1867 at Sitka.[3] Following the purchase, the Revenue Cutter *Lincoln* was ordered to Alaskan waters to map out our newest possession. It was typical of the multi-mission duties of the Service in that the *Lincoln* was transporting a group of survey men, the government's special agent and a surgeon[4]

Gold Rush (1848-1914)

On 17 July 1897, sixty-eight prospectors arrived in Seattle on the steamer *Portland*, every one of them rich. They became known as the Klondike Kings and their success started the Klondike Gold rush into the Yukon Territory. By the spring of 1898 there were 112 ships being built to meet the demand for passage to Alaska.[5] Many of these vessels were marginally up to the 1000-mile voyage.

The fact that there was gold in Alaska was well known. In 1880 Richard Harris, forty-six, and Joe Juneau, fifty-three, discovered veins of gold in the Silver Bow Basin in what is now the capital of Alaska, Juneau. Together they staked nineteen placer claims and sixteen lode claims. This started the first significant gold rush.[6]

---

3   ibid, 96

4   U.S. Coast Guard Public Information Division, *Bering Sea Patrol and Alaska Veterans History The Lincoln – U. S, Revenue Cutter.*

5   Cohen, *The Streets Were Paved With Gold*, 3

6   Borneman, 147

Gold Rush Impact on the Revenue Cutter Service

The influx of thousands of prospectors into Alaska presented challenges for the Revenue Cutter Service to maintain law and order. In one unique event the 207-foot sternwheeler *Nunivak* was detailed to maintain a year round presence on the Yukon River. The goal was to maintain law and order in what was a wild and lawless place.

Herein are two examples of the uniqueness of the Coast Guard's functionality. The Yukon River runs a long way from the sea, over 2000 miles, 600 of which are in Canada, yet the Revenue Cutter Service had jurisdiction over the U.S. portion. Its principle objective was one of law and order. Another interesting coincidence was that the commanding officer of the *Nunivac* was First Lieutenant John Cantwell who had a long history with Captain Hell Roaring Mike Healy, the great Arctic sailor. Healy is the namesake of the USCG Icebreaker *Healy* and he figures prominently in the next section on reindeer. The Yukon froze over in the winter, and the *Nunivac* would be allowed to freeze up to be ready next season. The crew did military drill on the frozen river to stay active during the long boring winter. This duty continued for four years from 1898 to 1902.[7]

Crew of the R/C *Nunivac* doing military drill on the frozen Yukon

7   Noble and. Stronbridge, *Captain "Hell Roaring" Mike Healy*, 114

Another early involvement was the Lifesaving Service station in Nome, established in 1905. Nome had its own gold rush of sorts when gold was discovered in the sands of fifty miles of the beach. This easy access was too irresistible to thousands of prospectors. By 1905 Nome's population had swelled from a few hundred to 25,000 inhabitants.[8] The coastal waters off Nome are very shallow and the anchorage for vessels is two mile out. That meant that passengers and cargo had to be ferried ashore in often very dangerous conditions. The original station was destroyed by a fire in 1934 and not rebuilt. During its operational time it was the northern-most station in the Service.[9]

Through Alaska to the Canadian Gold

Several of the major strikes, including the one that resulted in the Klondike Kings, occurred in Canada. This fact was lost on the thousands who rushed north to Alaska. It was not lost on the Canadian Mounties who waited at the borders to collect customs on what was brought in and taken out. In 1885 came the Forty Mile strike on the Stewart River. The Klondike rush was attributed to the Rabbit Creek strike that was filed in August of 1896. By the spring of 1897 there were 1,500 people living in Dawson at the junction of the Klondike and Yukon Rivers. But many more were coming. Between July of 1897 and early 1898, 50,000 prospectors stampeded north. [10]

To get to the Canadian gold fields the hopeful prospectors had to pass through Alaska if they came by water. This did much for the growth of Alaskan cities. The Canadians also required every prospector to have a grubstake of a years worth of food and equipment, which amounted to 2,000 pounds of beans, bacon and flour.[11] Probably one of the most vivid images of this frenzied craziness is the picture of the line of miners climbing up the Chilkoot Pass out of Skagway. At the top of the pass were the Canadian Mounties enforcing the customs laws. Most of the

---

8   Borneman, 209

9   Dr. Dennis L Noble, *Alaska and Hawaii,* 15-6

10   ibid, 174-6

11   ibid

prospectors were carrying their supplies on their backs, which meant many trips up the treacherous route involving 1,200 steps cut into the ice. It is estimated that 30,000 men, women and children made the attempt.[12]

The White Pass Route was somewhat longer but was not so steep allowing the use of packhorses and other animals. In the blind rush to get to the fields, anything that could walk was pressed into service. Many were cruelly over loaded and the White Pass Route became known as Dead Horse Trail.[13] For those who could pay the ferryboat fare, the Yukon River was the easiest route to the riches. This means to the bonanza became known as the rich man's route.

The most gold to be taken from an area came from Fairbanks. This discovery in 1904 required specialized high-pressure hydraulic mining, as the ore was deep. The Fairbanks Rush nevertheless caused the population of Alaska's second largest city to swell from a few scattered settlers to 5,000 people. From 1902 to 1914, sixty-three million dollars in gold was mined.[14]

Gold In Modern Alaska

Gold and other precious commodities are still being mined in Alaska and it ranks sixth of all states for mining value at $2.5 billion production. The difference today is that most of the money being made is by residents. The great majority of miners during the gold rush era were here to get what they could and then get out. It didn't matter if they left environmental devastation in their wake or not. In 2009 the Alaskan mining industry employed 2,126 people at an average salary of $91,100. Three quarters of these were residents.[15] As I write this, my own son who is a journeyman electrician in Alaska is wiring a new barracks for the Kensington mine near Juneau. He enjoys life in the historic capital city and hiking around the former gold digs and mines of the area.

---

12   Cohen, *Paved With Gold*, 50

13   Borneman, 181

14   ibid, 217

15   Alyssa Shanks, Mali Abrahamson, and Liz Baron, Economist, *Alaska Mining Industry*, (Juneau, Alaska Economic Trends, October 2010) 5-7

Reindeer

Despite what Santa says, reindeer are not indigenous to Alaska. Caribou are, but they are not reindeer. Nevertheless, reindeer were an integral part of the establishment of a Native based industry and year round food supply which saved several villages from extinction. What is likely news to most is that the Revenue Cutter Service was largely responsible.

Alaskan Reindeer Principals

The zealot missionary Shelton Jackson and the hard drinking Revenue Cutter Service Captain Mike Healy formed an unusual pair. Together, however, they were heroes in the history of the Alaskan Native people. Jackson did not embody the principle of the division of church and state. In fact in 1890 he was both a Presbyterian missionary and the first General Agent of Education for the U.S. government in Alaska. At the time Jackson was fifty-six years old. He was just over five feet tall but was nonetheless a giant in Alaska. During his lifetime he was to travel over a million miles and establish 100 missions and churches. These included the Native Indian schools in Alaska.

I don't know how tall Mike Healy was but in 1890 he was a great presence in the Arctic. At fifty-nine years of age he had been sailing the dangerous waters of Alaska since 1868. During the time of the importing of the reindeer he was the Captain of the R/C *Bear*. Jackson and Healy had become friends while Jackson was being transported on the *Bear* to do his federal education agency duties. Both men shared a deep concern for the plight of the Alaskan Native people. [16]

The Natives lived a subsistence lifestyle, which meant they gathered their year-round food supply when it was available. If they missed the opportunity to gather, they starved. Healy had found entire villages wiped out from the effect of alcohol brought by the whalers for trade. The unfamiliar alcohol resulted in incapacity to harvest, hence death by starvation for many.

---

16   Noble, *Healy,* 172-77

Captain Mike Healy

Jackson and Healy had seen what they thought was a solution when they crossed the Bering Straits to visit the Chukchi Siberian natives. Healy had gone there to present $1,000 in gifts to the Siberians for assisting a shipwrecked American sailor. The Chukchi had a year-round food and clothing supply in the form of domesticated reindeer that they had been cultivating for 3,000 years. Together Jackson and Healy discussed, "Why not the Alaskan Natives." Using his political connections and powers of persuasion, Reverend Jackson was able to obtain approval from Congress for the project, but no funding (does that sound familiar?). Undaunted he turned to the Presbyterian woman's organization and convinced them to fund the project yielding, over two thousand dollars to purchase reindeer.[17]

Captain Healy, using his cooperation with other agencies' authority, and strongly believing in the program, agreed to provide the transportation for the project. Healy's reputation and high regard by the native people greatly assisted in convincing the Chukchi herders to part with their precious reindeer.

---

17   Borneman, 131

The Reindeer Project

The first year of the project, 1891, saw the purchase of only sixteen head and the necessary moss to feed them. It is fantastic to picture a bunch of sailors hobbling these nearly wild, horned reindeer, transporting them by small boat alongside the *Bear,* and then hoisting them aboard by sling and block and tackle. But they did. The first winter they took them to Unalaska Island, location of Dutch Harbor. Despite concerns about how the reindeer would react aboard ship, they did well and did not panic in the unfamiliar surroundings and rolling decks. [18]

The news the next spring was not so good. None of the reindeer had survived the first winter. Reportedly this was because they ran out of the lichen/reindeer moss, and the animals starved. Undeterred, Jackson successfully obtained federal funding, again persuaded Healy and the *Bear* to assist him, and on 4 July 1892, 171 reindeer were landed at the new Teller Native School at Port Clarence. This was to become an Independence Day for the Alaska Natives.[19] Over the next decade, 1,100 reindeer were established at various native schools started by Reverend Jackson.

The Natives and the Reindeer

The program taught the natives how to tend to the reindeer. After a period of several years apprenticeship, the native herders were given reindeer to start their own individual herds. A reindeer apprenticeship required five years of tending and learning. Each apprenticeship was given two females and their offspring per year. At the end of the five years the new herder was loaned enough reindeer to make a herd of fifty. The loan was repaid as the herd grew. The program was not without its difficulties. The Siberian herders didn't work well with their Alaskan counterparts. Jackson was able to recruit Scandinavian reindeer herders with a long tradition of reindeer herding to come with their families to the Alaskan school herds and impart their knowledge.

---

18   Strobridge and Noble, *Alaska and the U.S. Revenue Cutter Service*, 54

19   ibid, 79

The discovery of gold at Nome in 1898 gave a big boost to the entire reindeer industry. Not only was there a need for more meat but also the reindeer were superior animals for logistics as they could pull sleds fully loaded with gear. They also were used for postal service, delivering the mails to the isolated communities. By the beginning of WWII, Jackson and Healy's experiment had grown to over a half a million animals.[20]

World War II in Alaska
Visiting a Battle Field
I vividly remember my introduction to Dutch Harbor. It was 23 May 1974 and I was co-pilot of HH-3F 1496 on a search and rescue (SAR) case to hoist a Japanese commercial fisherman from a fishing boat. This poor soul had a fishhook in his eye and we successfully performed a routine hoist from the fishing vessel, routine except the grateful crew had sent up a bottle of scotch with the patient in his litter. We then flew to Dutch where a commercial medical evacuation plane, paid for by the Japanese, took the injured passenger to Anchorage.

I had some time to look around Dutch while our helicopter was being refueled. It was like going back in time. The hills were loaded with caves and old gun revetments. These no longer held the anti-aircraft guns but still had the barricaded walls. I'd never been on a modern battlefield before. I learned later that Japanese carrier aircraft had bombed where I was standing during World War II. It was fascinating in a strange way. It wasn't until later that I learned about the Aleutian Campaign, which has become known as the "Forgotten War." As I learned more of the Aleutian campaign of WW II it became more and more fascinating to me. I also was to learn how little of this terrible struggle is known outside Alaska.

Fighting a War in Alaska
As the history of warfare goes, the section on Alaska is fairly recent. In fact a little over seventy-five years ago there weren't

---

20   ibid, 358

many military men who knew much about warfare in Alaska. One who did was Brigadier General William L. "Billy" Mitchell. On 11 February 1934, Mitchell was invited to testify before the House Committee on Military Affairs. The subject was Alaska and the importance of constructing air bases to defend it. He said in part:

> *"Japan is our dangerous enemy in the Pacific. They won't attack Panama. They will come right here to Alaska. Alaska is the most central place in the world for aircraft and that is true either of Europe, Asia or North America. I believe in the future, he who holds Alaska will hold the world, and I think it is the most important strategic place in the world."*[21]

Later in Mitchell's career he was one of the first to realize the importance and potential of aircraft in war, and he was not afraid to voice his opinions. In fact his outspokenness led to his being convicted by a General Court Martial in October 1925. The court was comprised of eleven major generals, including Douglas MacArthur.[22] He was subsequently found guilty of conduct to bring "discredit on the military service" for, among other things, criticizing the air defenses of Oahu, Hawaii in the press, much to the displeasure of the Hawaiian Commander, General Summerall.

Despite General Mitchell's lack of military tact he was recognized as a great strategic thinker; this was why he was being asked for his congressional testimony. Congress, however, did not follow his advice and did little to prepare for the defense of Alaska, our "top cover for America." The Territory was ill prepared when war did come. In fact the majority of military personnel in Alaska at the start of the war were Coast Guard personnel, not Defense Department personnel. Despite the Coast Guard's experience with operations in Alaska, we were not ready to defend it when World

21   Garfield, 49

22   Costello, 92

War II began. But, we were not alone. The nation was nearly dealt a knock out punch in the Pacific by the tragically successful Pearl Harbor attack on 7 December 1941. For twenty years leading up to this point the spirit in the country was one of isolationism and unpreparedness for self-defense. [23]

War With Japan
On 26 July 1941 in an effort to make the Japanese withdraw their troops from Indochina, President Roosevelt declared an embargo on all oil destined for Japan and froze Japanese assets in the U.S. It had long been acknowledged by military strategists that such a move would strangle the Japanese and could be a war starter. The strategists were right.[24]

Four months later, 360 aircraft launched from six different Japanese carriers struck Pearl Harbor on Sunday 7 December 1941. In a little over two hours, the U.S. Pacific fleet suffered a fateful destruction of eighteen warships, including eight battleships, three light cruisers, three destroyers and four auxiliary ships. In addition 188 aircraft were destroyed and our nation endured the loss of over 3,500 killed or wounded military casualties. The Japanese lost nine fighters, fifteen dive-bombers, five torpedo bombers, and five midget submarines with lives lost totaling less than 100. In one of the few fortunate circumstances for the U.S., all three of our remaining fleet carriers in the Pacific, the *Enterprise,* the *Lexington*, and the *Saratoga* were all away from Pearl Harbor. The *Yorktown* in the Atlantic fleet, and the *Hornet* under construction were key players later in the Pacific war. General Mitchell, who had passed away 17 February 1936, had once again been proven right by history.[25]

When the war started, there were slightly more than 25,000 people in the entire Coast Guard. This number was to experience a ten-fold increase to 180,000 during the war with another 51,000 in the temporary reserve. Almost half of these were afloat and

23   Garfield, 48

24   Prange, *At Dawn We Slept*, 168

25   ibid 539

participated in most theaters of the war including Alaska and the Aleutians.

Alaska Was Not Ready

The sole Department of Defense members in Alaska in 1940 consisted of approximately 300 soldiers in the Chilkoot Barracks in Skagway. The territorial governor Ernst Gruening had this to say about the installation:

> *Chilkoot Barracks had about as much relevance to modern warfare as one of those frontier Indian-fighting posts from the days of Custer and Sitting Bull. It had no road or air connection with the outside world. Its only transportation was provided by a 51-year-old harbor tug. When we went up the Lynn Canal, the terminal fjord of the Inside Passage, we encountered a 30-knot headwind that stopped us cold and stranded us for three days. We had to be rescued by the Coast Guard. If war had come, we'd have had to sue for peace and ask for a wind-check.*[26]

The Navy Alaskan presence consisted of 216 personnel and twelve patrol planes assigned to a seaplane station at Sitka on Japonski Island, and a Naval radio station at Dutch Harbor.

Alaska's infrastructure was also limited. There was no land tie with the outside world. The 80,000 people who lived in the state depended on the sea and air for their support. The railroad consisted of stretches between Seward and Fairbanks and Skagway to Whitehorse. Roads were almost nonexistent. As the war clouds gathered on the horizon, Congress slowly began to move. The first major project to be funded for Alaska was four million dollars for a cold weather test station at Fairbanks authorized in the

---

26   Garfield, 50

1940 budget. This was to be Ladd Field dedicated on 4 September 1940.[27]

Alaskan Buildup

General George Marshall, then head of the Army, lobbied for money for an airfield outside Anchorage. Congress wanted to include the Army's authorization with the Navy for a large $8.7 million base on Kodiak Island then being built. General Marshall was able to convince them that this was impractical because of the limitation of useable land and the mountainous terrain. Finally in 1941 twelve million dollars was authorized for the field that was to become Elmendorf Air Force Base on the Alaskan mainland at Anchorage. The clearing of the site began 8 June 1940 and the first contingent of 780 soldiers arrived two weeks later. This was the largest number of soldiers sent to Alaska up to that time.

One of the most significant things that happened in, and for, Alaska during the war was the tremendous amount of construction that was completed. Included were the 1,500 mile long Alaska-Canada Highway, the Whittier tunnel and Naval Bases at Kodiak and Dutch Harbor. Airfields were of critical necessity, and between 1940 and 1942 runways were constructed at Annette Island, Yakutat, Anchorage, Fairbanks, Nome, Naknek, Cold Bay and Otter Point. Other places that saw major military installations were Ketchikan, Juneau, Haines, Skagway, Cordova, Valdez, Seward and many others less known. As the war moved out into the Aleutians, fields were constructed under unbelievable conditions. The first was a secret field on Umnak Island, build under the cover story that is was to be a cannery. Another was constructed at Cold Bay. The strip at Adak was operational in only two weeks. Bases at Atka, Shemya, Amchitka, Kiska and Attu followed as the war progressed. WW II altered Alaska more than any other event.[28]

---

27   Garfield, 52

28   ibid, 65

The Coast Guard Contributes to the Build Up
The Coast Guard participated in the buildup by providing logistic support and our traditional navigational duties. The Service was also responsible for one of the "Black Box" miracles of the war, the Long Range Aids to Navigation or LORAN. Now largely taken for granted, back then the navigational accuracy provided to our ships and aircraft was considered almost magic and critically important.

LORAN works by a Master station transmitting an electronic signal from its 600-foot tower. This signal, when received by one or more slave stations, in turn transmits a signal. These signal are plotted on navigational charts as parabolas. By measuring the time difference in receipt of the different signals a ship can accurately calculate its position. LORAN, which had been developed by scientists at MIT in 1941, was field tested in 1942.

To build the chain in Alaska a 140 man Coast Guard construction battalion was established. In all they build eight stations in Alaska and the Aleutians. The construction, under battle conditions, and compounded by the Aleutian weather, was unimaginably difficult. The cutters *Cedar, Citrus* and *Clover* all participated at one time or another in the construction. The work was rugged and dangerous. While constructing the station at Attu, a bulldozer slid over a cliff, killing its Coast Guard operator. In all a dozen lives were lost during the projects.[29]

The first chain consisted of LORAN stations constructed at St. Matthew, Saint Paul, Umnak Islands, Saint George and Cape Sarichef. Late in the winter of 1943 a second chain was built in the Aleutians. Sites had been selected by a Coast Guard aircraft survey in August. Stations were selected at Adak, Amchitka and Attu. On 15 November 1943 a Coast Guard aircraft used in site work was lost. Flying from Port Heiden to Kodiak the plane was never heard from again. The wreckage was finally located in 1987 on a 3,000-foot cliff, 150 miles west of Kodiak. Remains and personal effects were recovered with the aid of Coast Guard helicopters.

---

29   Fern Chandonnet Ed. *Alaska At War 1941 -1945,* (Fairbanks, University of Alaska Press, 2008) 129-30

War Leadership in Alaska

During the critical buildup Lieutenant General Simon Bolivar Buckner, US Army, was the military boss in Alaska as the Commander of the Alaska Defense Command. His worst fears about defending Alaska with his meager force came true in the middle of 1942 when the war came to Alaska. While still a Colonel, Buckner had been selected for the Alaska job while Chief of Staff of the 6th Army headquartered in San Francisco. He held the Alaska command for four years from the frenzied build up days in July 1940 to the quieter times of June 1944. He was reassigned to command the 10th Army in its drive to Japan. He died in action during the Battle of Okinawa on June 18, 1945 and was never to fulfill his postwar dreams of settling on his farm in Homer and entering Alaskan politics. [30]

In charge of the Navy in Alaska was Captain Ralph Parker, USN. He had been designated as Commander, Alaskan Sector of the Seattle Naval District in October 1940. As such he was responsible for Alaska's entire coast. This was impossible as his naval assets consisted of one Navy ship, the U.S.S. *Charleston*. At the time of Pearl Harbor, he was the head of the Navy and Coast Guard in Alaska as the president had transferred the Coast Guard into the Navy on 1 November 1941. His fleet had grown by two old destroyers, two Coast Guard Cutters, and several converted fishing boats whose identifying numbers began with "*YP*." They soon became known as "*Yippee boats*".[31]

The Tide of the Pacific War Turns

Despite the fact that part of Alaska was to be lost to the Japanese for nearly a year, the month of June 1942 is considered to be when the tide of the war in the Pacific turned in our favor. Up to this time the Japanese had been having one success after another. They had, prior to the Pearl Harbor attack, expanded their East Asia "Sphere of Prosperity" into Manchuria, China, Mongolia and French Indochina, and island groups of the Carolinas, Mariana's

---

30   Borneman, 368

31   Garfield. 61

and Marshall's. With the U.S. fleet drastically weakened, Japan had nearly clear sailing. Singapore was taken, as was Hong Kong. After a catastrophically bungled beginning, the Philippines were brilliantly defended by MacArthur until April 1942. The loss of the Philippines was a foregone conclusion after an unbelievable lapse of readiness in which nearly all of MacArthur's 307 aircraft were caught on the ground, and destroyed by Japanese air only nine hours after the attack on Pearl Harbor. Japanese victories in Borneo, Celebes, Java, Rangoon, and Burma followed. It seemed that the giant plum of Australia was next on the limb to be cut off, and that the Japanese were unstoppable. Then came Special Aviation Project One.

The Doolittle Raid and Alaska

On 18 April 1942, one of the most bizarre operations of the war, the Doolittle raid, began. Sixteen Army B-25B medium bombers took off from the carrier *Hornet*, destination Tokyo. Coincidentally, the bomber used was named for General "Billy" Mitchell (probably the first time an aircraft has been dedicated to a person convicted by general court-martial). The Doolittle raid was audacious but an amazing gamble. We committed two of our precious carriers, the *Hornet*, under the command of Rear Admiral Marc Mitchner, and the *Enterprise* the flagship of the overall commander Admiral William "Bull" Halsey. President Roosevelt, however, felt the country desperately needed a victory.

What he got was probably a tactical failure but a tremendous strategic success. Tactically we lost all sixteen of the B-25s and twenty percent of the eighty-aircrew men that flew them. The damage inflicted, including a bomb through the deck of the carrier *Ryujo* in port in Tokyo Harbor, was minor. Strategically, however, the Japanese were stunned that their homeland could be attacked. The military leadership changed their priorities. Plans for isolating Australia were put on hold, and ADM Yamamoto's plan to trap and eliminate the U.S. fleet was approved. The Japanese didn't know where the land-based bombers came from. Speculation was that they had to come from the Aleutian Islands, lending support for their own audacious plan to attack the Aleutian Islands.

Japan's AO Plan
The Yamamoto plan to destroy the remaining Pacific fleet was a bold, complex and extensive concept. Known as the "AO" plan it involved 200 ships, including eight carriers and over 700 aircraft divided into eight task forces. The centerpiece was the taking of Midway Island.[32] While the plan was brilliant, in 20/20 hindsight it violated at least four of the generally accepted principles of war. "Economy of force" was not followed as the Japanese divided their forces. The "simplicity" principle was certainly violated. Eight task forces were spread over thousands of miles of oceans, with different objectives, all requiring split second timing. Finally "security" and "surprise" were lost because we had broken the Japanese code.

It seemed to Yamamoto that the Aleutian thrust was good strategy. It would divert attention and perhaps resources from Midway. It would also prevent the Allies from using the Aleutians to launch Doolittle type bombing missions at the home islands. Whatever the pros and cons, on 3 June 1942 the war came to Alaska.

Alaskan Navy
The head of the Navy for the entire Pacific was Admiral Chester Nimitz. He was aware of the thinness of the Alaskan defenses. However, there wasn't much he could do. After Pearl Harbor and the battle of Coral Sea the U.S. Pacific Fleet had no operational battleships and was down to two operational carriers and the damaged *Yorktown*. Admiral Nimitz was reluctant to split his few assets, but he wanted to give General Buckner something to defend Alaska.

As a compromise, Nimitz detailed Rear Admiral "Fuzzy" Theobald to command a nine ship North Pacific Force that sailed from Pearl Harbor on 21 May 1942. Theobald's forces consisted of five cruisers and four destroyers. They arrived at Kodiak on 27 May 1942.[33] One week later all hell broke loose in the Aleutians.

32   Prange, 98-106

33   Garfield, 13

At the time there were 45,000 American servicemen in Alaska, of which only 13,000 were on either the Alaska Peninsula or the two defended Aleutian Islands, Unalaska and Umnak.[34]

Attack in the Aleutians

In May and early June of 1942 the Japanese executed their complex plan to try and finish off the U.S. Pacific Fleet. A portion of the plan called for an attack and invasion in the Aleutian Islands. It will probably be forever debated whether this was a brilliant move or a great blunder for the Japanese. What difference the two carriers and aircraft sent north might have had at Midway will never be known.

At 0540 on 3 June 1942, seventeen carrier-based enemy aircraft bombed Dutch Harbor, Alaska. These planes, and how they got there, is part of one of the most complex, bizarre and little known episodes in the history of World War II. The Aleutian portion of Yamamoto's plan involved the Second Carrier Strike Force consisting of the light carriers *Ryujo* and the *Junyo* carrying eighty-two aircraft. The carriers had a covering force of four battleships. Two related task forces involved three escorted transports with 2,400 troops and a support group of two heavy cruisers. The plan was to strike by air at the installations at Dutch Harbor on 3 June. This was intended to draw the U.S. fleet north while the main Japanese force hit Midway on the 4th. On the 6th, Japanese amphibious landings were to be made at three locations, Adak, Kiska, and Attu. [35]

In port at Dutch harbor during the attack were six combatant ships including the Coast Guard Cutter *Onondaga*. She was a 165-foot Patrol Gunboat built in Bay City Michigan in 1934. During the attack her crews took the Japanese under fire expending 2000 rounds of anti-aircraft ammunition. While there were fifty U.S. casualties, the damage to the Dutch Harbor facilities was considered light.

One of the attacking Japanese finest fighting aircraft, the Zero, had an oil line shot out and made a forced landing on a small

---

34   Simon Ridge, *War In The Outposts*, 22

35   Garfield, 3-4

island before the engine seized. The pilot mistook the marshy flat area on the island for a safe place to land and the plane flipped in the soft tundra breaking the pilot's neck. The aircraft was only slightly damaged and its recovery for analysis was a great intelligence coup in the war.[36]

Following the Dutch harbor raids, the carriers headed west to cover the amphibious landings at Attu and Kiska. The landing at Adak had been called off because of extreme weather conditions. After its defeat at Midway, the Japanese claimed that the real objective had been the Aleutians invasion. U.S. citizens reacted with great alarm when it became known that there were enemy forces on U.S. territory for the first time since the war of 1812. Plans were soon started to build up forces in Alaska to retake the islands. Alaska became the scene of a number of significant events associated with the war.

Alaskan Coast Guard Contributions

On 9 July 1942, the USCGC *McLane* WSC 146, a Coast Guard 125-foot "Buck and a Quarter" under the command of Lieutenant Ralph Burns was credited with engaging and sinking a Japanese submarine with depth charges in Southeast Alaska. The sub had been sighted on the surface by a fishing vessel and first attacked by a Royal Canadian Air Force plane operating out of an air station on Annette Island. CG *YP 251* assisted the *McLane*, a converted fishing boat commanded by Lieutenant Neils Thompson. Both Thompson and Burns were awarded Legions of Merit medals for their successful operation. [37]

An operation involving the Coast Guard that was not so successful involved a troop transport USS *Arthur Middleton* APA 25. In preparation for retaking Attu and Kiska the buildup in the Aleutians had been greatly stepped up. A critical part of this was the bombing of the Japanese invaders and the prevention of their re-supply. In order to bring aircraft closer to the islands it was decided to occupy and build an airfield on Amchitka Island,

36   Garfield, 44

37   Leahy, 129

which was only seventy-five miles from Kiska and 240 miles from Attu. The *Middleton* was manned completely by Coast Guard personnel. It had been ordered to Kulak Bay on Adak to on load 3,200 Army troops for the Amchitka operation. On 12 January 1943, while offloading these troops at Amchitka, one of the infamous Aleutian Williwaws, Alaska's famous sudden bursts of wind that can reach 110 knots, came up and drove the *Middleton* hard aground. The crew and cargo were successfully put ashore in rubber rafts, but the ship stayed aground for eighty-four days where she became a favorite target for float equipped Zeros that flew from Kiska. Amazingly, although the *Middleton* was attacked frequently for nearly three months a bomb never hit her.[38] Also during the Amchitka storm, a Navy Destroyer was forced on the rocks and was lost. Coast Guard personnel participated in the rescue of 175 crewmen for which five Coast Guardsmen received the Navy and Marine Corp Medal for bravery.

Retaking the Aleutians

An interesting sidelight to the Alaskan/Aleutian war was the classic personality clash that involved the senior Navy Commander, Rear Admiral Theobald and Major General Buckner. In the initial stages of the Alaskan theater the Army and Navy were at odds about how to proceed. Theobald was reluctant to risk his few assets, and Buckner had no direct authority over the Navy.[39] Rear Admiral Thomas Kincaid finally relieved Theobald in January 1943. Kincaid and Buckner were of a like mind and got along famously. This was the combination that commanded the retaking of the Aleutians. [40]

The decision was made to invade Attu first, leapfrogging over the more heavily defended Kiska. The Attu invasion was known by the code name Operation Landcrab.[41] Typical of things Alaska when decisions are made by those unfamiliar with its challenges,

38   Leahy, 128

39   Garfield, 15

40   ibid, 166

41   Borneman, 359

the operation was scheduled to take only three days based on the numbers of troops involved on both sides. On 4 May the invading force of thirty-four ships sailed from the marshaling point at Cold Bay. Included were two battleships, the *Pennsylvania* and the *Nevada*. The original D-Day was to be 7 May 1943 but weather delayed it until the 11th.[42] The 15,000 troops met little opposition at the beach. The mountains on the other hand presented unprecedented dangers.

In General Buckner's words the Japanese could only be dug out with "corkscrews". The Attu battle was bloody. The U.S. lost 549 killed and 1,148 wounded. Over 1,200 U.S. forces suffered severe weather related injuries. Of the Japanese, only twenty-nine of the 2,400 soldiers were taken alive. Before the final battle their doctors gave 400 wounded soldiers fatal shots of morphine.[43] Attu was the first island infantry amphibious operation of World War II. It was also second only to Iwo Jima as being the bloodiest. Unfortunately, there are few who even know it happened.

Based on the experiences of Attu, plans went ahead to retake Kiska, code name Operation Cottage. It was scheduled for 15 August 1943.[44] The bombing built in intensity, and U.S. and Canadian planes dropped over 4,500 tons of bombs. The Eleventh Air Force used all of its 359 combat aircraft in the operation. One of the worst enemies was as always the Aleutian weather. During the Aleutian campaign the Eleventh Air Force flew 3,609 missions. There were forty aircraft lost due to combat and 174 due to weather.[45] For the Japanese however, the weather turned out to be an ally. On 28 July 1943 the Japanese fleet slipped through the U.S. blockade and successfully evacuated all 5,183 troops. Unaware that the island had been evacuated, the U.S. and Canadian combined operation was launched on 15 August. Involved were 100 ships and 34,000 troops. Remembering the

---

42   ibid, 358

43   Garfield, 263

44   ibid, 291

45   ibid, 328

Attu high ground strategy of the Japanese, the lack of opposition to the landing was not unexpected. The invasion continued. In the fog of war, twenty-five allied troops were killed by friendly fire or booby traps. Another thirty-one were wounded. The destroyer *Abner Reed* struck a floating mine and sank with the loss of seventy crewmembers.[46]

For the remainder of the war Alaska became the forgotten theater. Attu was greatly built up with 15,000 Army and 1,800 Navy and Coast Guard personnel. Ten-hour, 1,600 mile round trip bombing missions were launched against the Japanese northern islands. With the Japanese evicted however, the big news of the war was elsewhere. The Aleutian war was largely forgotten, except by those who fought there. It was nevertheless one of the most complex, difficult and interesting of the Pacific campaigns. The "Thousand Mile War" as it became known, required great courage and dedication to conquer the dual enemies of dedicated fighters and weather. This portion of our history is undeniably remarkable, and to ascribe it as "the forgotten war" is to do an injustice to those warriors of both sides who made the ultimate sacrifice there.

The Worst of the Worst: The Good Friday Earthquake, 27 March 1964

Earlier in the "Dangers" section I spoke at length of Alaska's history with earthquakes. The Good Friday quake was the worst of the worst. It originally was classified at 8.6 on the Richter scale but has since been revised upwards to 9.2. It is the most powerful earthquake to ever hit North America.

The 1964 quake released ten million times the destructive power of the Hiroshima atomic bomb and was felt 700 miles away. It dramatically changed Alaska not only physically, but also psychologically. Nearly every coastal community was impacted. Some such as Valdez and Kodiak were completely leveled. The death toll from the quake and resulting tsunami was 131, with 115 of those in Alaska.[47] Although containing an unprecedented

---

46 ibid, 268

47 *Alaska Almanac 31st edition*, 63

level of destructive force, the event could have been much worse in human lives lost. It occurred at 1736 (5:36 P.M.) so children were out of school and many people were home from work. The military in Alaska was instrumental in the recovery providing urban search and rescue, heavy equipment, airlift of supplies and emergency medical care. Seventeen C-123 aircraft took off at dawn on the following day carrying relief supplies to damaged communities. Over the next twenty-one days more than 3.7 million pounds of cargo was airlifted and distributed to hard hit areas.[48] In all it was an event that showed how vulnerable and yet resilient the people of Alaska are. I had my own small experience with this event.

A Good Friday Earthquake Story
My first encounter with things Alaska reached me in the warm waters of California on 28 March 1964 while assigned to the Coast Guard Cutter *Pontchartrain*. The *"Pontch"* was a 255-foot Ocean Station Vessel and had been my duty assignment for eight months following graduation from the U. S. Coast Guard Academy in New London, Connecticut.

The U.S. Coast Guard Academy
The Academy is the smallest of the service academies. Another distinction is that selection to attend is based solely on a national competition with no congressional or regional quota. The result was that the USCG Academy is one of the most selective four-year universities in the nation. At the time of my tenure only men attended. That changed in 1975 with the entrance of the first woman. The pendulum has swung full travel as I write this; a woman is the new Superintendent of the Academy.

Following graduation in June of 1963, all ninety-three of my classmates were assigned to cutters, buoy tenders or icebreakers, and we all went to sea. This had long been tradition, intended to give all Academy officers a common background whether we were eventually going to be aviators, engineers, marine inspectors or

---

48   Cohan, *8.6*, 90

whatever career path we chose. Another benefit of the US Coast Guard Academy is the training sailing ship *Eagle* on which cadets make two long cruises, usually to Europe, and two short cruises during their four years at the Academy.

USCG Academy sailing ship *Eagle*

The Admiral Calls

This particular evening, I was standing the in-port Officer of the Deck (OOD) duty. When not at sea or in a shipyard, all Coast Guard cutters keep approximately one quarter of the crew on board to be able to prepare the vessel to get underway in an emergency. The person in charge of the ship, in the absence of a more senior officer, is the Officer of the Deck. Generally these duties are routine such as requiring a check of mooring lines and seeing that the onboard crew are doing their duties.

The Quartermaster of the Watch received a phone call and answered, "Coast Guard Cutter Pontchartrain, may I help you?" A very serious voice on the other end said "This is the District Commander, let me speak to the Officer of the Deck." He quickly called me and said "The Admiral is on the line." Receiving a phone call from the Rear Admiral in charge of the Eleventh

District was like getting a phone call from the president. The Admiral said in a very business-like manner, "There has been an earthquake in Alaska and a tidal wave is heading down the West Coast. Get the ship underway as soon as possible and proceed to a safe anchorage."

The *Pontchartrain* captain had always taken the ship in and out of port himself. Accordingly, even though I had been aboard for three quarters of a year, I had never gotten the ship underway before, which caused me some concern. We had practiced docking and getting under way on some harbor tugs at the academy, and I had watched the old man do it many times so I was sure I could handle it. I directed a recall of the crew and the onboard personnel were organized to start making the necessary preparations for getting the ship underway. Just as I was about to order the mooring lines cast off, the Operations Officer came running up the pier and he actually took the vessel to sea about an hour after the phone call from the District Commander. The Captain arrived by small boat several hours later where we were anchored.

The Alaska Quake's Impact on the West Coast
Fortunately on that Saturday evening in March of 1964 the impact on the Long Beach and Los Angeles area harbors was minimal. Not so up the coast in Crescent City, California. Starting just before midnight and continuing through the early morning hours of 28 March, a series of four waves hit this coastal community with devastating results. Ten people were drowned and property damage was estimated as high as sixteen million dollars. The fourth wave reached a height of nearly sixteen feet above the high tide mark. There was an unbelievable amount of debris left behind when the water retreated. An estimated 2.5 million board feet of lumber had become flotsam, as had over 1,000 automobiles. People found fish in flowerpots and in desk drawers. The extensive port facilities were destroyed, and waters reached seven blocks back from the waterfront.[49]

---

49   Cohen, 8.6, 106

The tsunami's effects were felt along the Washington and Oregon coast as well, although not as dramatically as in Crescent City. In one story, a grandmother in Seattle heard of the possible tidal wave heading for the coast and called her daughter who was vacationing at Kalaloch Beach in Washington approximately one third of the way down the coast from the Straits of Juan De Fuca. The daughter raced to the beach where her own eleven-year-old daughter was sleeping in a tent with a friend. Grabbing the children by the hand they ran to higher ground where at an elevation of forty feet above sea level the first wave reached them up to their knees. The surge was especially dangerous because it carried huge logs along with it.[50] This was my introduction to Alaska and the earthquake and resultant tsunami that plagues it.

Oil and the Trans-Alaska Pipeline (TAPS)

There is no question that oil plays a major role in Alaska. The gold rush going on at the same period oil was discovered overshadowed it, but not for long. Early drilling for oil took place at Iniskin on the Kenai Peninsula in 1898. A few years later, wells were drilled at Katalla, fifty miles from Cordova. The oil industry in Alaska swung into high gear with the discovery of the Prudhoe Bay oil field north of the Arctic Circle. In 1920 Congress authorized oil and gas leasing. In 1923 the federal government created Naval Petroleum Reserve Number Four, now known as National Petroleum Reserve Alaska. The problem, as is often the case with Alaska's natural resources, was how to transport the resources to market.[51]

In 1969 the Coast Guard assisted in a complex experiment connected with the North Slope. My old ship featured in Chapter 11, the icebreaker *Northwind*, carrying two of the more capable HH-52A helicopters escorted the 1,005-foot icebreaking super tanker *Manhattan* in testing the feasibility of a transcontinental deep-water all-season tanker route through the Northwest passage. The *Manhattan* made two successful trips to the North Slope, but using

---

50   ibid, 113

51   Cohen, *The Great Alaska Pipeline*, 1-6

tankers was abandoned because of the expense of constructing them and the environmental risk. Three much smaller Coast Guard cutters had accomplished the first polar circumnavigation of the North American continent in 1957. These were the cutters *Storis, Bramble* and *Spar*. Although successful in the transit, the use of icebreaking tankers was not considered feasible. The escort of the *Manhattan* was one thing, but how did a nice organization like the Coast Guard get involved with oil spills?

Vessel Traffic System Valdez

Marine Safety Office Valdez has within its responsibilities the Vessel Traffic Service Prince William Sound (VTS PWS). The VTS system has as its purpose "to provide active monitoring, information services, traffic organization and navigational assistance for vessels in confined and busy waterways." VTS is similar in concept to Air Traffic Control for aircraft with one big difference. ATC has positive control of aircraft under instrument flight rules. A VTS however is advisory in nature, and the safe navigation of a vessel is always the responsibility of the captain of the vessel. The whole reason for the existence of this VTS in such a remote location as Valdez, Alaska was a result of the Trans-Alaska Pipeline System (TAPS) being built. TAPS is another of the Alaskan defining events. The authorization for construction of TAPS had been a political rocky road. A federal suit was initially brought to block its development by three environmental groups, the Wilderness Society, the Friends of the Earth and the Environmental Defense Fund, who sought to block the construction based on the fact that its planning had not followed the guidelines of the new National Environmental Policy Act (NEPA). After three years going back and forth in the courts, the ball was tossed to the U.S. Congress to decide.

The Trans-Alaska Pipeline

Again, feelings were strong on both sides of the issue. Senator Mike Gravel of Alaska attached an amendment that would prohibit further legal actions based on environmental issues against the TAPS project. The amendment vote was a 49 to 49 tie with Vice-President Agnew casting the deciding vote in favor of the amendment. The passage of the final bill authorizing construction was passed in October, aided considerably by public opinion following the OPEC oil embargo imposed on the U.S. following the Arab-Israeli War and our support of Israel. [52]

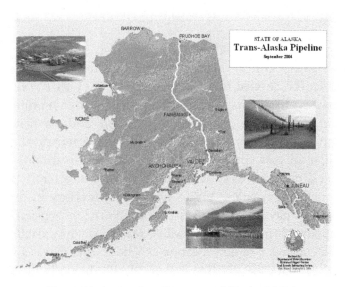

Trans-Alaska Pipeline (Courtesy of Alaska DNR)

The ultimate completion of TAPS was an amazing accomplishment. The construction took three years, employed 28,000 workers and cost $8 billion. In one of the biggest under-estimations in history, typical of things Alaska, the original estimate of the cost had been $900 million, about one tenth of the final cost.

Despite claims of a disastrous impact on the environment, the actual construction was done in a very responsible and sensitive manner. Everything about the TAPS is impressive. The pipeline is forty-eight inches in diameter and 800 miles long. A little less than half of the pipeline is buried; the remainder is above ground on

---

52   ibid, 19

78,000 supports located sixty feet apart. The supports are insulated so as to not thaw permafrost areas. Over 800 river and stream crossings were required. The entire pipeline was built to withstand volcanic activity and 151 stop flow valves are incorporated in its construction.[53]

Alyeska Pipeline Service Co. built the pipeline, which is a consortium of five oil companies:

- BP Pipelines (Alaska) Inc. (46.93%),
- Conoco-Phillips Transportation Alaska (28.29%),
- Exxon-Mobile Pipeline Co. (20.34%),
- Koch Alaska Pipeline Co, LLC, (3.08%)
- Unocal Pipeline Co, LLC (1.26%).[54]

The total cost of the TAPS, including the terminal in Valdez, was eight billion dollars. The first oil reached Valdez on 28 July 1977 and the first tanker full, on the *SS Arco Juneau* departed Valdez on 1 August 1977.

The oil companies are reaping serious profits, and the State of Alaska is being funded to the tune of about eighty-five percent of its budget through the royalties on the oil. The citizens of Alaska are also receiving a considerable benefit not only in the employment and support money but also through an ingenious reverse taxation mechanism known as the Permanent Fund [PF]. Established in 1976, the Permanent Fund was approved by an Alaskan constitutional amendment in which a dedicated fund of at least twenty-five percent of all mineral lease rentals, royalties, royalty sales proceeds, federal mineral revenue-sharing payments and bonuses was created. The principal of the PF can only be used for income-producing investments.

The Alaska Permanent Fund

In 1980 the Alaska Legislature established the Permanent Fund Dividend Program. Initially eligible residents were to receive

---

53   ibid, 33

54   *Alaska Almanac, 31st Edition*, 171

a fifty-dollar dividend for each year they had been a resident. This provision of the program was declared unconstitutional by the Supreme Court in that it established different classes of residents. In 1982 the program was revised in which an initial dividend of $1,000 was paid to each applicant who had lived in the state for at least six months. Dvidends in varying amounts have been paid every year since then.

In the first thirty years of the PF program over nine billion dollars in oil royalties have been invested. Through proper management and investments these deposits have grown to nearly $33 billion as of 30 June 2006. In excess of $14 billion in dividends have been paid out since 1982. Given that the population of the state has never exceeded 700,000, the per capita share has been a significant sum.

Alaska Statehood
When Secretary of State William Steward bought Alaska from Russia in 1867 there were thirty-seven states. Alaska did not become the thirty-eighth state but rather the forty-ninth, and that took ninety-two years. Why did it take so long? The problem was that most people felt the place was too cold, too isolated and too expensive. For years there was no law in Alaska because to have law you needed law enforcement. For seventeen years after its purchase, the military officers or customs collectors assigned to the capital in Sitka ruled Alaska. But they were few, and Alaska was huge.

Early Governing Models
The *First Organic Act* was passed in 1884, which led to the appointment of a token governor, John Kinkaid of Nevada and a single district court judge. The people of Alaska had no rights and no say in their governance such as it was.

Things improved somewhat with the passage of the *Second Organic Act*, which created the Territory of Alaska in 1912. The capital had been moved to Juneau in 1905 and the first Territorial Legislature convened there in 1913. This body had very limited powers and ninety-nine percent of the land lay under federal control. The President and U.S. Congress also controlled the natural resources and fiscal matters. Large outside concerns dominated Alaskan commerce with its chief exports of salmon, gold, and copper. The principle imports for the territory were petroleum, whiskey and tin cans for canning salmon.

Attempts at Statehood

The first statehood bill was introduced in 1916, and many more were introduced over the years only to fail to pass. Finally in 1955 Alaska formed a constitutional convention on the campus of the University of Alaska at Fairbanks. There were fifty-five elected delegates, forty-nine men and six women. One of the men was a Native Alaskan. The goal of the convention was to craft a model constitution with a strong executive, a balanced legislature and an independent judiciary. The Alaskan voters unanimously ratified the constitution and the Alaskan delegation was able to take the constitution in hand to petition Congress to finally approve statehood for Alaska. Congress did so in June of 1958, and President Eisenhower signed the *Alaska Statehood Bill* on 3 January 1959.[55]

Changes incurred in fifty years of statehood[56]

Item	1959	2009
Population	225,000	691,354
Percent of Land owned by Federal government	374 million acres (100%)	242 million acres (65%)
Native population	43,100	122,306
Most valuable export	Seafood	Oil & Gas

The Exxon Valdez Oil Spill

In 1989 the Valdez vessel traffic system had been operating for twelve years. In the previous year the six billionth barrel had arrived at Valdez and in May the 8,000[th] tanker load had departed. The experiment of the pipeline and Valdez Terminal operation had been a great success. This rosy picture all ended with the

55   Joseph Hardenbrook, coordinator, *Creating Alaska*, (Anchorage, University of Alaska, 2005)

56   Gates. *Alaska Almanac 32 Edition*, 9

grounding of the tanker vessel *Exxon Valdez* on Bligh Reef shortly after midnight on Friday 29 March 1989. There is no question in my mind that this was another of the defining events, a major layer of the Alaska onion. Many players got black eyes by this event, private, state and federal, including my cherished Coast Guard. The whole story is in the Marine Environmental Protection chapter.

Chapter Three

What's the U. S. Coast Guard

Describing the Coast Guard
The 2011 Coast Guard Snapshot

My primary intention in writing *Guarding Alaska* was to explain what the Coast Guard does. My hands-on experience ended with my retirement in 1993 after thirty years of active duty. The world changed after that. The terror of 11 September 2001 affected everything, especially the Coast Guard. The statutory duties haven't changed that much but priorities for the Service have changed dramatically. This information is current as of 2012:

- The U.S. Coast Guard is one of the five armed forces of the United States and the only military organization within the Department of Homeland Security.
- Since 1790 the Coast Guard has safeguarded our Nation's maritime interests and environment around the world.
- The Coast Guard is an adaptable, responsive military force of maritime professionals whose broad legal authorities, capable assets, geographic diversity and expansive partnerships provide a persistent presence along our rivers, in the ports, littoral regions and on the high seas.

- Coast Guard presence and impact is local, regional, national and international. These attributes make the Coast Guard a unique instrument of maritime safety, security and environmental stewardship.[1]

Coast Guard Statistics
- Enlisted workforce 33,200
- Officers 8,398
- Civilians 8,342
- Reserves 7,997
- Auxiliary 31,419
- 2011 Budget $10.1 Billion
- Shore locations 945
- Ships 247
- Boats 1,850
- Aircraft 204

The People of the Coast Guard
The active duty Coast Guard is roughly the size of the New York Police Department, but law enforcement is just one of its dozen duties. It is largely male at 84.3%, however the last two Vice Commandants (number two officer in the Service) have been female as is also the Superintendent of the Coast Guard Academy. The head of the Coast Guard is the Commandant, a full admiral (four stars). The Commandant serves for a four-year term.

The Service has five vice admirals (three stars) and thirty-nine rear admirals (two stars and one stars). One of these rear admirals is in charge of Alaska. The Coast Guard Auxiliary is comprised of civilian volunteers who assist the active duty in a number of ways. With a membership of 31,000 they are nearly as large as the active duty.

---

1 USCG Public Affairs, *2011 Coast Guard Snapshot.*

Organizational Structure

The Commandant and his staff are in Washington D.C. There are two area commands: Atlantic, headquartered in Norfolk, Virginia and Pacific, headquartered in Alameda, California. Each is headed up by a vice admiral. There are nine districts under the area commands. Alaska is District 17 and is within the Pacific Command along with District 11 (California, Nevada, Utah and Arizona), District 13 (Washington, Oregon, Idaho and Montana) and District 14 (Hawaii) (the numbering systems for districts followed the US Navy system and over the years districts have been combined and eliminated so there are gaps.) Subdividing the nine districts are 35 sectors.

Sectors of the Coast Guard

Sectors are new to me, but they seem like a good idea. The first sector was established in Miami in 2004. Alaska has two sectors, Juneau and Anchorage. Sectors provide unified response for all Coast Guard responsibilities in a geographical region and are tailored to the maritime operations in the sector. They are responsible for Captain of the Port duties, Marine Inspection responsibilities, Federal On Scene Coordinator duties in the event of a pollution incident, and SAR Mission Coordinator responsibilities. [2]

Defining the Coast Guard
History

1789:

- 7 August – The Lighthouse Service established under the control of the Treasury Department.[3]

1790:

- 4 August – Alexander Hamilton created the Revenue Marine Service in the Treasury Department, including authorization for ten cutters to be constructed.[4]
- 21 March – Hopley Yeaton is commissioned as "Master of a Cutter in the Service of the United States for the Protection of the Revenue," signed by President George Washington. Yeaton is the first officer of the Service, and his remains are entombed adjacent to the Memorial Chapel at the U.S. Coast Guard Academy.

1801:

- Revenue Cutters render outstanding service during the Quasi War with France.

1812:

- Fleet of Cutters is ordered into action as an arm of the U.S. Navy in War with the British.

---

2   Captain Joe Vojvodich, *Look at Sectors, Building upon Authorization Capabilities, and Partnerships*, USCG Academy Alumni Bulletin, December 2011, 41-44

3   Kaplan and Hunt, *This Is The Coast Guard*, 57

4   ibid, 2

1831:

- Cutter *Gallatin* is directed to cruise the coast in search of persons in distress. Start of search and rescue.

1836-39:

- Seminole Indian Wars, during which Cutters operate with ground forces along coast of Florida.

1845:

- 19 February – Lighthouse Service is transferred to Revenue Marine Service.

1848:

- Lifesaving Service begins.

1861:

- 12 April – Cutter *Harriet Lane* fires first naval shot in Civil War in Charleston Harbor.

1910:

- 9 June - *Motorboat Act* is passed. This act was the first statute to address safety on motorboats. The act dealt primarily with navigational lights and sound signals, and required motor vessels to carry life preservers and fire extinguishers.

1912:

- 14 April - *Titanic* sunk by iceberg. International Ice Patrol started in 1914 by international agreement. Coast Guard is given responsibility to carry it out.

1915:

- 28 January – The Coast Guard is formed by combining Revenue Cutter Service and Life–Saving Service.

1917:

- 6 April - USCG became part of the Navy for World War I, with fifteen cutters, 200 officers and 5,000 enlisted involved.

1918:

- Cutter *Tampa* in a convoy from Gibraltar to Milford Haven, Wales blows up with loss of all 155 hands. During World War I, the Coast Guard sustains the highest rate of losses of all American services.

1919:

- USCG is assigned responsibility for enforcing prohibition at sea, and the"Rumrunner War" ensues.

1932:

- 31 March – US signs *Whaling Convention* with 21 other nations, and USCG assigned enforcement responsibilities.
- 2 May – *Northern Pacific Halibut Act* passes and again the USCG given enforcement responsibility.

1936:

- USCG is assigned ice-breaking responsibility by executive order.

1939:

- CG "Reserve" is established as an all-volunteer, non-military force to assist recreational boaters; name changed to Coast Guard Auxiliary in 1941.
- Lighthouse Service is incorporated into USCG bringing with it 29,606 aids to navigation.

1940:

- President Roosevelt invoked the *Espionage Act of 1917* and the USCG is assigned the Port Security mission.

1941:

- 19 February - CG Reserves is established as a military component of the Service.
- Cutter *Northland* makes first American capture of the war, the Norwegian trawler *Boskoe* with German radiomen.
- 9 April – U.S./Denmark defense pact signed for Greenland, and USCG is assigned to patrol area.
- 1 November–USCG is once again transferred to Navy.
- 8 December – War is declared with Japan following Pearl Harbor attack and during the war Coast Guard gains peak strength of 214,000, 90% of which are reservists.[5]

1942:

- 28 February – Bureau of Navigation and Steamboat Inspection is transferred to USCG.
- 25 November - SPARs established (CG Woman's Reserves). "SPARS is formed from first letters of Coast Guard motto, Semper Paratus, Always Ready."

1944:

- 29 June - Helicopter lands on USCG Cutter *Cobb*. The CG is given the responsibility to develop use of helicopters in anti-submarine warfare (ASW) and search and rescue (SAR).

1956:

- 10 May-Public Law 519 is passed, bringing all previously uninspected vessels on U.S. waters carrying more that six people for hire under USCG regulations.

---

5   Rear Admiral David Callahan, "Coast Guard Reserve – 71 Years of Service To America", (*Coast Guard Compass*, 14 February 2012)

1965:

- 24 July-Navy requests CG Cutters for Vietnam service. Cutters are assigned as well as aids to navigation teams, teams, port security units and dangerous cargo handling units. (Thirty-six of my classmates from '63 serve in Vietnam.)
- 24 July – Navy turns all icebreakers over to the USCG.

1967:

- 1 April – President Johnson transfers USCG into newly formed Department of Transportation.

1970:

- 3 April - *Water Quality Improvement Act* broadens CG authority for pollution and cleanup efforts.
- Traditionally the Coast Guard had patterned its uniform after the Navy. That changed with Admiral Bender who was Commandant of the Coast Guard from 1 June 1970 to 1 June 1974. Among his many accomplishments, he is best remembered for the distinctive uniform he decreed the Coast Guard personnel should wear, which became known as the "Bender Blues".

1971:

- 10 August - *Federal Boating Safety Act* gave CG wider authority over recreational boating in U.S.

1973:

- National Strike Force is established to combat oil spills. These three Strike Teams are air transportable teams established on the east coast, gulf coast, and west coast.

1976:

- 1 April - *Fisheries Conservation Management Act* (200 mile limit) initiated.

1985:

- 16 November – HH-65A Dolphin helicopter enters the Service.

1990:

- March - HH-60J Jayhawk helicopter enters the Service.
- August – *Oil Pollution Act of 1990* is enacted.
- 17 August – Coast Guard boarding teams are committed to Operation Desert Shield.

2001:

- 11 September – World Trade Center Twin Towers and Pentagon are attacked with hijacked commercial passenger jets.

2003:

- 1 March – USCG is transferred into Department of Homeland Security with 21 other agencies and becomes the third largest governmental agency with 200,000 employees.
- At the height of Operation Iraqi Freedom (2003-2011) 1,250 CG personnel, two high endurance cutters, a buoy tender, eight patrol boats, four port security units and support units are assigned to the war effort.

2004:

- 12 July - First Coast Guard Sector is established in Miami FL.[6]

2007:

- 23 July – The consolidated acquisitions directorate is instituted in the Coast Guard to handle major systems and future equipment acquisition.

---

6   Vojvodich, 40

2010:

- 20 April – "Deep-water Horizon" explodes causing loss of life and a massive oil spill. Coast Guard leads response to first "Spill of National Significance". Admiral Thad Allen, while still Commandant, is appointed as President's personal coordinator.

Chapter Four

The Coast Guard in Alaska

The Coast Guard has been in Alaska since before its purchase from Russia in 1867. Deciding it would be pertinent to determine what we had purchased, the Revenue Cutter *Lincoln* was detailed to chart and explore our new possession. The *Lincoln* was the first of many famous cutters to be involved with Alaska through the Alaska Patrol and the Bering Sea Patrol.[1] The modern Coast Guard in Alaska is a far cry as far as capabilities but the challenges are still there.

Seventeenth CG District Statistics2
- Active Duty Military   2,203
- Civilian employees   401
- Auxiliary   480
- Operating Budget $313 million
- Acquisition, construction $29 million
- SAR cases (2009)   666
- Aids to Navigation   671

---

1   USCG Headquarters Public Information Division, *Bering Sea Patrol and Alaska Veteran History The Lincoln – U. S. Revenue Cutter.* 2001

2   D-17 Public Affairs, *The Coast Guard in Alaska 2010.*

Coast Guard History in Alaska

1867:

- US purchases Alaska from Russia for 7.2 million dollars. A lighthouse was already established in Sitka in the cupola of Baranof Castle. Revenue Cutter *Lincoln* transports government personnel and begins surveying Alaska.[3]

1884:

- Lighthouse Service establishes fourteen iron buoys and a beacon light in Sitka Harbor.

1889:

- Revenue Cutter Service begins patrolling the coast for the protection of the salmon fisheries.

1890's:

- Revenue Cutters enforces fur seal harvesting in the Bering Sea. Tensions arise between U.S. and Great Britain. R/C *Corwin* seized British steamer *Coquitlan* for illegal sealing for which a fine of $600,000 is paid.

1891:

- R/C *Bear* transports the first of the reindeer to establish herds at Native school.

1899:

- R/C *Nunivak* is assigned to the Yukon River for a four-year period during the frenzy of the gold rush to enforce law and order.

---

3   Dr. Dennis Noble and PA1 Barbara Vouigaris. *Alaska and Hawaii, a Brief History of U. S. Coast Guard Operations*, (Washington D. C., USCG Historians Office, May 1991) 1-18

1900-1905:

- Congress authorizes $100,000 to build eleven lighthouses in Alaskan waters.

1903:

- 18 June - Scotch Cap Light is established at Unimak Pass. It is Alaska's first coastal lighthouse.

1905:

- Lifesaving Service establishes a station at Nome Alaska during the gold rush boom.

1940:

- 23 November - Ketchikan is selected as the headquarters for the Coast Guard in Alaska. Following the end of WW II, headquarters for Alaska Coast Guard is repositioned to Seattle.

1947:

- 17 April – Coast Guard Air Detachment is established at Naval Air Station Kodiak consisting of one PBY seaplane, seven pilots, and 30 crewmembers.

1948-9:

- Capital city of Juneau Chamber of Commerce petitions CG Headquarters in Washington D.C. to re-establish District Headquarters in Juneau. Ketchikan also made a bid for it to be located in their city. A rivalry developed between the two cities. Both Chambers sent delegations to CG Headquarters in Washington D.C. Juneau is eventually chosen when they offer to provide a headquarters building funded by private donations. Excavation of the Construction started on 14 April 1949. The keys are turned over to the CG on 14 September 1949.[4]

---

4   The Daily Alaska Empire, September 14, 1949

Three story building in Juneau contains offices of the State of Alaska. It was originally build as Headquaters for the Alaskan Coast Guard.

1977:

- 19 April - Air Station Sitka is established having moved from Annette Island near Ketchikan. Housing built at Annette is barged to the new station. Station was originally intended to be helicopter and fixed wing. Determination made that the Falcon jet cannot be safely operated in Alaska and Sitka declared helicopter only.

1980:

- 4 October – The Holland America cruise ship *Prinsendam,* 150 miles from shore in the Gulf of Alaska, experienced an engine room fire that eventually requires abandoning ship. 519 elderly passengers and crew are rescued by an international effort of air and surface resources of Coast Guard, Air Force, Canadian and civilian vessels.

1982:

- 30 July 1982 – The C-130 CGNR 1600 crashes on Attu Island in the fog on a logistics/fisheries enforcement flight. There are two fatalities. Aircraft was strike damage meaning it is a total loss.

1989:

- 24 March – Tanker vessel *Exxon Valdez* runs aground in Prince William Sound Alaska causing a huge oil spill. Federal On Scene Coordinator (FOSC) was USCG. First FOSC is Captain of the Port Valdez, who is relieved by CCGD17 Commander Rear Admiral Nelson, and CCG Pacific Area Commander Vice Admiral Robbins eventually relieves him.

Chapter Five

What Does the Coast Guard Do?

I must admit that until entering the USCG Academy in July of 1959 I knew little of the Academy and what the Coast Guard was or did. Growing up in eastern Washington state my only afloat experience was running a water ski boat on the Columbia River. I had always been fascinated with the PT Boats of WW II and thought that would an exciting pursuit. I soon found out that neither the Navy nor Coast Guard operated PT Boats after World War II.

Coast Guard Academy New London CT

U.S. Coast Guard Academy

I learned about the Coast Guard Academy when Mr. Reed, my Richland High School counselor gave me a copy of a booklet *Take a Look at Your Future* that described the USCG Academy and how to make application. I was basically a 3.0 student in high school but I was a football player, student body VP, and active in my church, all of which helped my resume. I was also a good test taker. The Yakima Washington Postmaster conducted my interview, even though he had no experience with the Coast Guard. We got along well however and he must of given me a good recommendation. At any rate, of about 3000 applicants approximately 200 others and I were selected to enter the Academy in July 1959. Four years later, ninety-three of us headed to cutters, buoy tenders, and icebreakers around the country with our shiny new ensign bars on our collar.

The USCG Academy had its roots in the first Revenue Cutter School established on the topsail schooner *Dobbin* in 1876. After a stint at Fort Trumbull the Academy was moved to its present location in New London in 1932. The academy like the Coast Guard itself has had a complicated history regarding its duties.

An Alphabet of Coast Guard Terms

- **Aids to navigation** - Buoys, day markers, lighthouses, electronic aids; basically all marine traffic navigational systems.
- **Auxiliary** - Thirty-one thousand civilian volunteer arm of the Coast Guard family.
- **Armed Service** – the USCG is an armed service of the United States at all times.
- **Boating safety** – Major safety program including inspecting boat builders, approving personal flotation devices, recreational boat inspections.
- **Bridge administration** – the CG is responsible for the establishment and operation of all bridges over navigable waters.
- **Cutters** - All Coast Guard ships are known as cutters from the days of the Revenue Cutter Service. A Cutter is any CG vessel over sixty-five feet in length that crew

can live aboard. There are approximately 247 cutters at present. Cutters less than 179 feet in length are under the operational control of District Commanders. Cutters over 179 feet are under the control of Area Commanders in either Atlantic or Pacific.

- **Districts** - The Districts are nine geographical areas each headed by a Rear Admiral. The numbering is patterned on the Navy system. Alaska is CG District Seventeen. District Commanders are responsible for operations within their geographical boundaries.
- **Environmental Protection** - A key mission of the CG encompasses protection of whales, seals, and commercial fisheries in addition to protection of the environment from pollution.
- **Flexibility** - A USCG Principle of Operation. The others are Clear Objective, Unity of Effort, On-Scene Initiative, Effective Presence, and Managed Risk Restraint
- **"F"** - also stood for finance when I was on active duty. The budget for the USCG for 2011 was $10.1 Billion.
- **Guardians** - An unofficial title for members of the Coast Guard.
- **Homeland Security** - Agency home of the Coast Guard since 2003.
- **Icebreakers** -A specialized vessel designed to operate in the ice. The USCG is charged with operating all the national icebreakers.
- **International Ice Patrol** - has been operated by the CG ever since the loss of the *Titanic*.
- **Juneau** - Capital of Alaska since 1905 and the district headquarters of the Coast Guard in Alaska.
- **Ketchikan** - The first Alaska headquarters for the CG.
- **Law Enforcement** - The original purpose of the service was to enforce the customs laws of the United States.
- **Marine Safety** - A very broad mission that encompasses all aspects of the maritime industry including design

of US built ships, their construction and throughout their operating service. Licenses U.S. mariners.

- **Navy** - The Coast Guard becomes a specialized service under US Navy upon declaration of war or when directed by the President.

- **Ocean Stations** - During the early period of trans-oceanic flights Coast Guard operates a number of ocean stations in the Pacific (three) and Atlantic (ten) at the point of no return or midway. Navigational assistance was provided as well as rescue capabilities should an aircraft have to ditch. The US involvement in the program ran from 1930 to 1974. In this period before satellites weather observations made on patrol were important sources of forecasting information. These missions were alternately known as weather patrols.

- **Primary Duties.** The CG shall: 1) enforce or assist in the enforcement of all applicable Federal laws on, under, and over the high seas and waters subject to the jurisdiction of the US; 2) shall engage in maritime air surveillance or interdiction to enforce or assist in the enforcement of the laws of the US; 3) shall administer laws and promulgate and enforce regulations for the promotion of safety of life and property on and under the high seas and waters subject to the jurisdiction of the US covering all matters not specifically delegated by law to some other executive department; 4) shall develop, establish, maintain, and operate, with due regard to the requirements of national defense, aids to maritime navigation, ice-breaking facilities, and rescue facilities for the promotion of safety on, under, and over the high seas and waters subject to the jurisdiction of the US; 5) shall, pursuant to International agreements, develop, establish, maintain, and operate icebreaking facilities on, under, and over waters other than the high seas and waters subject to the jurisdiction of the

US; 6) shall engage in oceanographic research of the high seas and in waters subject to the jurisdiction of the US; and 7) shall maintain a state of readiness to function as a specialized service as part of the Navy in time of war, including the fulfillment of Maritime Defense Zone command responsibilities.[1]

- **Quick Response Guide** – Seventeenth Coast Guard District multi-agency procedures guide for handling an emergency on a passenger vessel. Goal is to Plan and Prepare Today To Prevent and Respond Tomorrow. See the *Prinsendam* rescue in chapter Twelve.

- **Reserve.** 7,500 member uniformed personnel contingent available to respond to mobilization as needed. At the peak of Operation Iraqi Freedom in April 2003, 4,400 reservists were on active duty. Special Port Security Units (PSU's) are equipped with air-deployable twenty-five foot armed boats. PSU's are only one of several Coast Guard Deployable Specialized Forces. Other units are Maritime Security Response Teams, Maritime Safety and Security Teams, Tactical Law Enforcement Teams, and Regional Strike Teams.

- **Search and Rescue (SAR)** – Assist persons and property in danger on the water. On an average day the Coast Guard responds to sixty-four SAR cases nationally saving twelve lives every day.[2]

- **Transportation** - Executive agency that was the Coast Guard's home from 1967 to 2003.

- **Treasury** - Prior to Transportation the Service was in Treasury from 1790 to 1967.

- **Unity of Effort** - One of the CG Principles of Operation and the reason that Groups and Sectors were created, to coordinate operations in a geographic area with an effective standardized response.

---

1   *U.S. Code*, Title 14, Part I, Chapter 1, art. 2

2   *2011 Coast Guard Snapshot*

- **Vessel Traffic System (VTS)** - A Coast Guard operated navigational monitoring system located in the major U.S. ports to provide traffic information to vessel transiting. There are twelve systems currently: Prince William Sound (AK), Puget Sound (WA), Valdez (AK), Seattle (WA), San Francisco (CA), Los Angeles/Long Beach (CA), Houston-Galveston (TX), Berwick Bay (LA), St Mary's River (MI), Port Arthur (TX), Tampa (FL) and New York (NY).

- **"W"** - The letter in the vessel designation that indicates that it is a Coast Guard cutter. Examples are WAGB – Icebreaker, WMSL – National Security Cutter, WHEC – High Endurance Cutter, WMEC – Medium Endurance Cutter, and WLB – Seagoing Buoy Tender, and WPB – Coastal patrol Boat. In all there are 24 cutter designations.

- **"X"** - Is the Navy Hull Classification Designation for a submersible craft. It is of concern to the CG as narco-submersibles have been used to smuggle drugs. These type craft were nicknamed *"Bigfoot"* because they were rumored to exist but had never been actually seen. In 2006 a *Bigfoot* was seized southwest of Costa Rico carrying several tons of cocaine. In 2008 reported sightings were occurring at a rate of ten per month but seizures were rare. Upon detection, the crew would scuttle the sub, which would rapidly sink[3].

- **YP** - During WWII in Alaska miscellaneous fishing vessels were placed in temporary service with the Coast Guard for coastal patrol. These were designated YP and became known as "Yippee boats." A Yippee boat actually sank a Japanese submarine in Alaska as told in Chapter Two.

- **Zero** - The designation of a Japanese fighter in WWII that was particularly effective against the Allied aircraft. A Zero was shot down during the

---

3   Wikipedia, Narco-submarine

Dutch Harbor Alaska bombing on 4 June 1942. Its impossible to determine who shot the plane down however the Coast Guard cutter *Onondaga* had put forth considerable fire from its shipboard guns. Military Preparedness is one of the Coast Guard's core missions and is detailed in Chapter Seven.

Illustrative Stories of Coast Guard Missions

To explain further what the Coast Guard does, why it does it and how, I will use my experiences and what I learned in Alaska as illustrations. Each of the following chapters will explain one of the Service's missions by telling a story involving that mission, explain what the statutory basis is for it, and then explain how it is accomplished in Alaska

There are many ways to look at the Service's missions but I will do so historically. What came as a surprise to me is that the oldest mission in the Coast Guard is law enforcement. When my classmates and I took our oath at the Coast Guard Academy in 1959 to begin our careers, we took a second oath as Custom Officers. We were joining the Treasury Department and not the Defense Department. Accordingly the first mission area I will discuss is Enforcement of Laws and Treaties (ELT).

Chapter Six

Enforcement of Laws and Treaties (ELT)

An ELT Story - The Crash of the HC 130H 1600

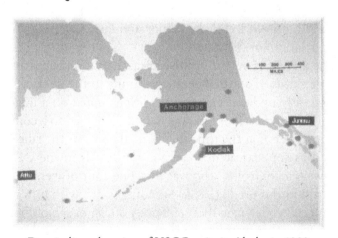

Dots indicate location of USCG units in Alaska in 1982

Day One As Chief of Search and Rescue
My first day on the job was 30 July 1982, a Friday. I remember it well because I had just relieved Commander Dick Shoal as Chief of Search and Rescue for the Seventeenth District covering Alaska and its waters. My new job title was North Pacific Search and

Rescue Coordinator (NORPACSARCOORD) with responsibility for a program covering 3.8 million square miles of ocean or an area larger than the continental United States. Dick was going to retire with his family to a ranch in Idaho following a few more months of active duty. My wife and family and I had just returned for our third tour in Alaska a week earlier from the Air Station/Group in North Bend Oregon. I'd also inherited a nice office on the Seventh Floor of the Federal Building in Juneau with a great view south down Gastineau Channel.

Dick and I spent the week familiarizing me with the responsibilities of the job. Fortunately, having been stationed earlier at CG Air Station Kodiak and on the icebreaker *Northwind*, I knew the geography and operations in Alaska. Coast Guard units at the time are depicted in the graphic. The main function of the Office of Search and Rescue (OSR) was to provide a twenty-four hour operations center (OPSCEN) that coordinated all Coast Guard operations in Alaska and its area of responsibility (AOR). The district commander at the time was Rear Admiral Dick Knapp class of '51, an old icebreaker-sailor and later Commissioner of Transportation for the state.

The OPSCEN was a beehive of activity even on a routine day. The status of all the operational units in the district had to be constantly updated and their positions noted on a huge wall chart. Later on much of this was to be transferred to a computer based system but at the time the manual plot was the rule of the day and as sophisticated as we got. On watch in the OPSCEN was always a controller who was a second tour officer, usually a lieutenant junior grade (LTJG) Standing watch with him was an assistant controller, usually a chief petty officer or senior first class petty officer. During my two years experience as OSR these were all males, although females would later join the team as women progressively moved into all of the different fields in the Service.

The controller and assistant controller were on watch for 24 hours and it was a high stress job. Part of the stress was caused by the requirement to brief the Admiral and his senior staff at 0900 every morning on the weather, status of units and ongoing operations. I was blessed with some top-notch young officers and petty officers during my tour. I was also lucky to have an outstanding assistant, Lieutenant Commander (LCDR) Bob Vail a black shoe seagoing sailor type, to balance out my own brown shoe (aviator) background. The black shoe brown shoe distinction has its own history.

The Navy uniform footwear in the olden days were low quarter; square toed black shoes which were fine onboard its coal-fired ships, because they did not show the soot. The early naval aviators, however, were training on dirt fields in San Diego. Accordingly their black shoes were always showing dust, and their superiors were constantly admonishing them. The first six flyboys decided that brown shoes and leggings would be less likely to show the dirt. They submitted a petition, which was approved on 13 November 1913. Brown shoes and leggings thereafter became the early uniform footwear for aviators.[1]

Following the week's checkout, Dick and I reported to our immediate senior, Captain Larry Telfer, the Chief of Operations, that we were ready for relief of the duties. He gave the transfer his blessing and I picked up a very complex bag of responsibilities. As it turned out I wasn't going to have them long.

A Missing C-130

Mid-morning on that Friday the controller called me in my new office and requested that I come in to the OPSCEN. I immediately did so and he briefed me that the Air Station at Kodiak reported that communications had been lost with one of their large four engine C-130's on the third day of a routine multi-missioned deployment known as the Adak-Attu Log. Log stands for logistics, which means they were carrying cargo and mail. This was a mission flown every several weeks that involved doing fisheries enforcement flights to locate the positions of the foreign fishing fleet along with logistical missions into Attu LORAN Station, a long-range electronics navigation station for mariners.

---

1   LCDR William L. Estes, USN (Ret) in a letter for the record. (www.thebrownshoes.org)

The Controller briefed me that the C-130H CGNR 1600 had departed Shemya Air Force Base on the Aleutian island of the same name for the thirty mile flight to Attu Island earlier that morning. The aircraft had not arrived at the Attu airstrip and the Commanding Officer, Lieutenant Junior Grade Smith called Kodiak to report his concern. Smith and part of his crew had been awaiting the C-130 at the airstrip. CGAS Kodiak ran its own operations center as a satellite to the Juneau District operations center. They had initiated various procedures to attempt to establish communications with the 1600. Several airborne C-130s had been diverted and told to proceed to Attu and try and contact the 1600.

The C-130H 1600, or Hercules as it was known, was a third generation C-130. The Service had approximately thirty-two C-130s in the inventory in 1982, four of them assigned to Kodiak Air Station. The "Herc" is so well designed for its function that it is still being produced. There had been 2,262 built up to 2006 and operated by fifty nations other than the U.S. The Coast Guard had never lost a Hercules. The C-130 as operated by CGAS Kodiak, was the very definition of a multi-missioned aircraft. Its cabin deck was a series of rails and rollers that were designed to accommodate cargo pallets. The payload of the H model is 45,000 pounds. It could also be rigged for special airline type seat pallets (rows of airline type seats mounted on roller pallets that could be quickly loaded or unloaded) to carry over seventy passengers. The Herc cruised at 292 knots, or about 334 MPH. It had a range of over 2,300 miles and was the perfect aircraft for Alaska as the Coast Guard did much of its own logistics supply work for far-flung stations.

I did what you usually do when you want to get the straight word. I called someone I knew and trusted at Kodiak, my old hunting partner, Commander Mike Stenger who was on his second tour at CGAS Kodiak, third in Alaska, this time as the Executive officer of the air station. When I got him on the phone, he said he had just heard about the situation and was heading down to the Rescue Coordination Center (RCC) in Hanger One to check it out.

Mike was concerned, as was I, because the C-130 was so reliable with many redundant systems. The Lockheed C-130 Hercules is a very dependable aircraft and had been in service with its original contractor, the U.S. Air Force, since December 1956. It had also been a workhorse for the CG entering service in 1959.

Casco Bay runways on Attu island, crash site lower left

Attu – A Different Sort of Place

Attu, figure (6-2) is a unique and remote place. It is one of the most isolated duty assignments in the Service. At the very end of the Aleutian chain it is approximately 1,200 miles from Anchorage. Attu lies at a longitude of 173 east. The International Date Line is bent around Attu so it is in the same time zone and date as the rest of the Aleutians. The island has a remarkable history for such an isolated outpost. During World War II Attu was one of two Aleutian Islands occupied for a year by the Japanese. Of importance here is the Attu weather, which greatly compounded military operations in World War II and was to complicate the search and rescue operations for the 1600. The average temperatures are not extreme by Alaskan standards, but typically windy, rainy, and cold; perfect hypothermia conditions. Attu is located at the juncture of the Bering Sea and the Pacific Ocean and the interface causes unstable weather and reduction of visibility due to fog is common.

At the time Kodiak Air was alerted that the aircraft had not arrived at Attu as scheduled, it was twenty-five minutes overdue. The Kodiak Rescue Coordination Center had immediately diverted an airborne C-130, the 1602 to proceed and had also requested the activation of the DOD Direction Finder Net. Communications were lost with the 1600 when they were en-route to Attu LORAN station transporting three passengers and about 500 pounds of cargo. Losing communications with helicopters in the Aleutians is not uncommon due to their low altitude. Losing contact with the C-130 with its more extensive communications equipment and normally higher altitudes was unusual.

C-130 with Barometer Mountain, Kodiak in background

Mission Background

This mission was combination logistics and law enforcement flown every two weeks. The normal plan was to be gone from Kodiak for three days with the aircrew staging out of either Naval Air Station Adak or Shemya Air Force Base, both of which were

DOD bases in the Aleutians. The flight usually landed at Attu every day delivering supplies, mail and personnel. In addition to delivering the beans, as logistics missions are called, the aircraft each day flew a mission into the Bering Sea to locate and broadcast the location of foreign fishing vessels to be used by Alaska Patrol Cutters enforcing the 200-mile fisheries management area.

These flights were known as ALPAT, or Alaskan Patrol flights. This information was crucial for the ALPAT cutters who were slugging it out in the normal lousy Aleutian weather. Their shipboard radar and sensors at the time only gave them about a 30-mile range for detection so that without the information provided by the ALPAT flights they were operating in the blind.

Day One

The 1600's mission began on 28 July 1982 when the aircraft departed Kodiak at 0730 with a crew of eight and twelve passengers. Among the passengers was a six-person USO band destined for Shemya AFB and Attu LORAN Station to provide entertainment for the Coast Guard and Air Force personnel stationed at these isolated locations. Shemya was the primary staging area for the Adak-Attu log as it was only thirty-three miles from Attu. At the time Shemya was a major Air Force installation involved in monitoring Soviet activities. Day one of the 1600's mission included a landing at Attu for delivery of supplies, the USO Band, and then landing at Shemya for the RON (remain over night). The day was largely uneventful.

Day Two

Day two began with a short flight to Attu LORAN Station to deliver supplies and to return the USO Band to Shemya. The aircraft was shut down and refueled. An ALPAT flight was then flown in support of the ELT mission and the 1600 recovered at Shemya. The most notable event of the day was the final landing, which was done in actual instrument conditions and required a ground-controlled approach (GCA) in which the aircraft was talked down to landing by way of precision radar. The weather also resulted in the cancellation of a planned logistics event into Attu.

Day Three

The third, and final day of the Adak-Attu Log and ELT mission was Friday, 30 July 1982. At 0630 the crew made preparations for the short trip to Attu. They loaded 500 pounds of cargo and briefed the three passengers for the flight. The passengers consisted of a machinist mate third class assigned to Attu, returning from emergency leave, a seaman apprentice reporting in to Attu LORAN, and a middle-aged female contract college instructor working at Shemya who was going to Attu to present a slide show on the Mt. St. Helen's eruption as part of a morale program.

The Weather

When the pilots first checked the weather at 0700 it was below minimums for the flight. Approximately an hour later the Aircraft Commander called the watch stander at Attu via a landline phone between the two islands. The watch stander reported that the weather was "pretty good" with a ceiling above 900 feet and that he could see landmarks that indicated the visibility was at least three miles to seaward. He failed to mention that there was a ring of fog off shore encircling Massacre Bay where the station was located. This was a serious omission.

In preparing for the flight the crew made several decisions that would affect the outcome of the mission. The crew was planning to land at Shemya after the logistics trip and had decided to not refuel the aircraft following the previous day's mission. The relatively light fuel load was fortunate as it turned out. Another decision made by the pilots that was not so fortunate was not to wait for the Inertial Navigation System (INS) to warm up. This system is similar to a GPS in concept and gave a fairly accurate position at any time. The 1600 departed Shemya at approximately 0810. The weather reported by the tower to the aircraft was ceiling 400 feet scattered, 1,000-foot variable broken, and 2,000 overcast with visibility of eight miles. Wind was from the southwest at twenty knots. The aircraft relayed to the tower that they would be requesting 20,000 pounds of fuel upon return from Attu.

En route and Arrival

En route the two pilots discussed the procedures for making the approach into Attu. Both pilots were in their third year of their assignment at Kodiak Air Station and were experienced with Alaska operations. The Aircraft Commander was also CGAS Kodiak's standardization pilot, which meant he was responsible for training other pilots. There were no aeronautical navigational aids to assist with the approach into Attu making it a visual flight rules (VFR) only facility. This required flying approaches clear of clouds with visual contact with the runway. The airport and runway for Attu is named Casco Cove. There is one primary runway 020/200 which is paved and 6300 feet long by 150 feet wide. The northern half is wash-boarded by frost heaves. The field is "For Official Use Only" and visual flight rules (VFR) only. Landing at Attu can be challenging because of the high terrain that surrounds the field.

With the reported wind out of the southwest the plan was to use the 200 runway. This required the aircraft approaching from the east to make a slight right turn at Alexai Point to follow the high terrain of Gilbert Ridge and then circle to land on runway 200. When visibility restricts the approach the weather radar is used to pick up prominent landmarks. The first of these points is Chirikof Point, the most eastern point of Gilbert ridge. The next landmark is Alexai Point, and the final checkpoint is Murder Point, which defines the western edge of the safe zone over water. The critical decision point was Alexai Point where, if the field was not in sight, a missed approach was executed by turning south to open water.

As the 1600 flight proceeded they found themselves flying into lower ceilings than expected. The Aircraft Commander descended to 200 feet in an attempt to stay visual and keep the surface in sight. Meanwhile the co-pilot and flight navigator were attempting to determine the position of the aircraft using the weather radar. At this juncture the situation seriously deteriorated. Not having the INS, the crew apparently mistook Alexai Point for the first critical reference of Chirikof Point. The crew proceeded towards the second point on the radar, thinking this was Alexai when it was actually Murder Point. Upon reaching what they thought was Alexai, the crew was still in the fog, literally and figuratively.

Crash site of 1600. Note the imprint in the tundra of the aircraft lower center

The Crash
Shortly there after, terrain was seen under the aircraft coming up fast. A hard banking turn to the left was initiated but it was too late. The aircraft impacted Weston Mountain at an altitude of approximately 300 feet. The imprint in the soft spongy tundra showed that the aircraft hit parallel to the terrain. This is known as pancaking in. (Figure 6-4). The fact that the gear was down and the aircraft was "dirty"(meaning gear down, flaps down), fifty percent flaps and a relatively slow airspeed, made it possible for the crash to be survivable but a terrible experience for those onboard.

Upon impact, the cockpit, with its crew of five, broke off and rolled up the mountainside for a distance. During the subsequent fact finding investigation, which I was senior member on, we located paint from the cockpit on rocks several hundred feet up the hill. Gravity took over after the momentum was lost, and the cockpit rolled back down, finally coming to rest on top of the burning wing. In the cargo compartment, seats tore loose with passengers in them. The wings sheared off. The tail section separated and ended up heading 180 degrees from the crash direction. The debris trail defined a circular pattern to the left following the terrain.

Personnel and Crew Injuries

There were eleven crew and passengers. Nine survived, but with serious injuries. Two personnel, the scanner trainee and the seaman reporting into Attu LORAN, both eighteen years old, perished in the crash or the fire that followed. All of the survivors were very seriously injured, some critically. The five crewmembers in the cockpit included the aircraft commander, a lieutenant, who received a broken knee, multiple bruises and cuts to his head and a dislocated big toe. The co-pilot, also a lieutenant, received a broken nose, head injuries and a fractured mid-back. Sitting between the two pilots was the flight engineer, a petty officer second class. He received a dislocated and broken right arm and injuries to his head and right leg.

The navigator was a third class petty officer. He was trapped by the wreckage and was freed by the two pilots. He received burns over much of his body and had an unstable spinal cord injury that resulted in paralysis from the neck down. He was the most seriously injured of the survivors and was declared in a death imminent status twice during his hospitalization. The fifth crewmember in the cockpit was the radio operator, also a third class petty officer. He received a fractured back that initially resulted in paralysis.

The four survivors in the cargo bay included three third class petty officers made up of the loadmaster, one of the scanners, the Attu crewmember returning from leave and the 58-year-old female civilian college instructor. The loadmaster broke both ankles. The drop master also had a fractured ankle.

The pilot and co-pilot managed to get everyone clear of the cockpit by exiting the overhead hatch, which was now laying only a few feet from the ground. The remaining four survivors either found themselves outside the remains of the aircraft or were able to exit on their own. They now faced an additional problem in that no one but the civilian naturalist were dressed adequately for the cold, wet, hypothermic conditions. Additionally the intense fire caused by the burning fuel was consuming most of the survival gear. By an incredibly fortuitous stroke of good fortune, the co-pilot found a survival sled, which had been thrown clear and was able to retrieve the emergency locator beacon and activate it. He placed it on part of the wing that the survivors were huddling under.

The Uncertainty Phase

The "uncertainty" phase of the 1600 crash commenced when the watch stander at Attu reported to Kodiak Air Station and Shemya AFB that the aircraft was twenty-five minutes overdue. The Rescue Coordination Center (RCC) at Kodiak had alerted the Department of Defense Direction Finding (DOD-DF) net and diverted an airborne Coast Guard C-130, CGNR 1602 to proceed to Attu. Shemya diverted an airborne KC-135 Stratotanker to also head to Attu. This aircraft was the first to pick up the emergency beacon signal that had been activated by the co-pilot.

An additional favorable circumstance was that a Coast Guard Cutter, the high endurance cutter *Mellon*, was on Alaska Patrol with an embarked HH-52A helicopter, 1425 (similar to the one in figure 6-5). The *Mellon* was only eighty-five nautical miles northeast of Attu at the time of the crash.

HH-52A landing on Coast Guard Cutter

Back in Juneau at the Alaskan headquarters for the Coast Guard we made the decision to take SAR Mission Coordinator (SMC) responsibility for the case due to the rapidly expanding scope of agency and unit involvement. The *Mellon* was diverted and directed to Attu at best speed. At this time we didn't know if the 1600 had crashed on land or in the water. Naval Air Station Adak was requested to launch a P-3, a large four engine maritime patrol aircraft to listen for the 1600.

USCGC *Mellon*, a 378" High Endurance Cutter

The Rescue Team

On board the *Mellon* (figure 6-6), the Commanding Officer, Captain Marty Daniel, later Vice Admiral and Pacific Area Commander, made the decision to not launch the helicopter until they were within fifty miles of Attu because of poor weather in their vicinity - visibility of one mile in rain squalls and wind from the southwest at fifteen knots. *Mellon* went to flight quarters and launched the HH-52 at 1150 approximately three and a half hours after the crash. The weather at launch was still poor with a ceiling of 100 feet and visibility of one-quarter mile in fog. The two pilots were experienced Alaskan pilots, Lieutenant Bill Peterson, and co-pilot Lieutenant Mike Wallace.

As the helicopter was feeling its way towards Attu, Kodiak launched another C-130 with a medical team headed by Dr. Marty Nemiroff, a Public Health Service Flight Surgeon and expert on cold weather survival. The H-52 arrived in the vicinity of Murder Point at approximately 1240. By this time they also were receiving the emergency locator transmitter (ELT) and began homing in on it. In the words of the pilots they flew the helicopter like "an all terrain vehicle" slowly hover taxiing up the mountainside, homing in on the locator signal. At approximately the 200-foot level they spotted the first of the survivors.

The Rescue
The co-pilot of the helicopter, Mike "Waldo" Wallace fortunately was a qualified emergency medical technician (EMT). He volunteered to be lowered to the crash site and began triaging the survivors and readying them for transportation. Lt. Peterson, and the hoist operator Petty Officer Second Class Jeff Smith began transporting survivors to the LORAN Station.

Crash site looking down slope. The tail section on the left side of picture had rotated 180 degrees from the impact direction

LORAN Station personnel along with visiting USAF active duty personnel rushed to the scene via tracked vehicles and on foot to assist with moving the survivors. Peterson and Smith flew the first five of the most seriously injured to the *Mellon*. The helicopter needed to be refueled before flying on to Shemya AFB. Fortunately the Air force had provided a large cargo KC-

135 specially configured for medical evacuation dispatched from Elmendorf. At Shemya, Dr. Nemiroff supervised the stabilization of the survivors. At approximately 1550 LT Peterson flew back to Attu to pick up the remaining survivors for transport to Shemya.

The USAF medical evacuation aircraft departed Shemya at 2045 and landed at Elmendorf shortly after midnight, roughly 16 hours after the crash. The survivors were transported to the USAF Elmendorf Hospital. The fact that the eight badly injured personnel were transported from a mountainside in one of the remotest parts of Alaska to a hospital bed 1200 miles away, in survivable condition and in a relatively short time, was nothing short of miraculous.

Why Does the Coast Guard Enforce Laws and Treaties?

The Coast Guard had as its original purpose enforcement of customs laws. A better question might then be, why does the Coast Guard do anything else? I hope to answer that in later chapters. By law, the Coast Guard has eleven missions. Of these eleven, four are directly related to enforcement of laws and treaties; Drug Interdiction, Living Marine Resources, Migrant Interdiction and Other Law Enforcement. There are three additional mission areas that have a heavy law enforcement component that will be covered under the Marine Safety chapter. These three mission areas are: 1) Ports, Waterways, and Coastal Security; 2) Marine Safety; and 3) Marine Environmental Protection.

The Coast Guard has a challenge enforcing United States laws on the high seas, inland waters and the Great Lakes. The traditional name of this function is Enforcement of Laws and Treaties or ELT. ELT is the oldest of the Coast Guard's missions.[2] Added to these original law enforcement duties has come an assortment of unusual tasking's. In 1919 came prohibition and the Service was charged with stopping the "rum runners." On 31 March 1932 the U. S. signed the *Whaling Convention* with twenty-one other

---

2   *USCG History Program, "USCG Missions Timeline: Law Enforcement"*, 1

nations, and the CG was given the responsibility of enforcement[3]. Perhaps the largest increase in law enforcement responsibilities came in 1976 when the *Magnuson-Stevens Act* was passed. It created the 200-mile economic enforcement zone, or EEZ, thus greatly expanding the Coast Guard's fisheries enforcement areas.[4] In Alaska the EEZ area to enforce is greater than all the rest in the US combined.

A presidential order was signed in 1981 authorizing the Coast Guard to stop vessels suspected of carrying illegal migrants bound for the United States. This is not a big job in Alaska, but it's a huge one for the Seventh District in Miami. All of this law enforcement tasking has resulted in one of the nicknames for the Coast Guard - *Smokies of the Sea.*

ELT in Alaska

The Revenue Cutter Service a.k.a. Coast Guard's law enforcement mission was active in Alaska even before it became a US territory enforcing the sealing treaties in the Pribilof Islands. It soon included all of Alaska and the 200 Aleutian Islands. In Alaska the primary focus of the ELT mission is enforcement of the fisheries laws on waters over which the U.S. has jurisdiction or treaty authority. This is a very complex and important business in some of the harshest conditions in the world. Again politics compounds the difficulty by influencing what priorities are put on this enforcement. When the focus of the President and the national media is on stemming the flow of illegal drugs coming into the Southeast of U.S., Coast Guard resources follow.

Alaska is fortunate that for years its political representative held key power positions to ensure that Alaska fisheries enforcement was not short of resources. When I was originally stationed at Kodiak Air Station in the early 1970's, it was a common occurrence at night to see the lights of hundreds of foreign fishing vessels off shore. These were primarily Russian and Japanese fishing fleets that were pulling in thousands of metric tons of the ground fish

---

3   ibid, 2

4   ibid, 2

with their bottom trawls. There were frequent occurrences of the foreign fleet trawling through U. S. fisherman's crab pot lines and the resulting loss of crab gear.

The 200 Mile Limit (FCMA)

The *Magnuson-Stevens Fishery Conservation and Management Act* (FCMA) passed in 1976, resulted from the concern of the U.S. fishermen of the impact of unlimited foreign fishing in nearby waters. The FCMA has become known as the 200-mile limit and has established eight regional fisheries management councils for conservation and management of all fisheries within federal waters. The council responsible for Alaskan waters is the Northern Pacific FMC. Membership of the Northern Pacific FMC includes eleven voting members; six from Alaska, three from Washington, one from Oregon, and the Alaska Regional Director of the National Marine Fisheries Service. In addition there are four non-voting members, one each from the USCG, U.S. Fish & Wildlife Service, the Pacific States Marine Fisheries Commission,and the U.S. Department of State.[5]

Prior to this act, the U.S. had jurisdiction of the territorial sea out to only three miles. The 200-mile limit defined federal economic enforcement zone (EEZ) waters as between three and 200 miles. This resulted in a tremendous increase in the amount of ocean the USCG, as lead enforcement agency, was now responsible for. The EEZ in Alaska is over 900,000 square miles. Enforcement of fisheries laws is a complex undertaking. The fishermen are most notably not U.S. citizens so there is always the concern of impacting international relations. Back in the days when the cold war was hot in Alaska this could get interesting. For the most part the host countries were cooperative and were more punitive with their own countrymen who were found to be breaking the law then we were.

---

5   *Alaska Fish & Wildlife News,* "The North Pacific Management Council: What Is It? (www,we,adfg,ak,us/index.cfm?adfg+wildlife_news. view, 12/2007)

Doing the Enforcing

Vessels were required to log in a certain area to fish for a prescribed species and a specified amount. Infractions that were common included fishing in the wrong place, or under-logging the catch. The allowable harvest was all based on a quota system to guarantee a sustainable harvest. Enforcing the areas was a straightforward process. Normally HC-130 long-range patrol aircraft, such as the 1600, would fly patrols and determine the location of the fishing fleets. This info would be passed to cutters of the Coast Guard who were assigned fisheries patrol for up to sixty days at a stretch. These cutters routinely carried an aviation detachment (AVDET) flying an HH-52A Sikorsky helicopter or more recently the HH-65 Aerospatiale Dolphin helicopter.

It Isn't Always Easy

Determining whether or not a fishing vessel was in the correct area was fairly simple. Ascertaining whether or not they were keeping accurate books was much more complicated. The process involved putting a USCG boarding party on board each fishing vessel to examine the fisheries logs. The fish count was based on physically examining the catch. On board the fishing vessel the fish had been gutted and headed and then quick frozen in blocks. The boarding officer would pull a number of these blocks and weigh them until they had a statistically significant average weight per block. Based on the configuration of the ship and its refrigerated holds a fairly accurate estimate would be made of the number of blocks of fish being stored. Multiplying the number of blocks by the average weight per block, the catch logs than could be audited in a reasonable manner.

The boarding officer knew that his determinations would need to be sufficiently accurate to withstand the scrutiny of a subsequent legal process. If violations were serious enough, an immediate recommendation would be made from the enforcing vessel to the operational commander back in Juneau that the vessel be seized. This would start a process that involved the state department, the parent country, as well as the District Commander's team of law enforcement and legal experts talking with their counterparts in the Area Office in Alameda, California and even at the Headquarters level back at Buzzards Point in

Washington D. C. This process was sufficiently defined so that a decision could be reached in a matter of hours. If the vessel was seized it would be towed into port, usually Kodiak, where the catch could be offloaded and more formally disposed of. This was necessary because the process of determining what fine to assign or other sanctions to pursue could take several weeks in the legal system and the onboard fish had to be processed.

Dixon Entrance
An additional component of the ELT mission is enforcement of the disputed border area known as Dixon Entrance. The controversy hinges on the fact that when Alaska was purchased from Russia, the boundary in Southeast Alaska between Canada and the new territory was not agreed upon, and has never been clarified between the two nations. The U.S. position is that the boundary is a straight line between two points known as the A-B line. The Canadians on the other hand contend that the boundary should be a line drawn to three miles seaward from the high water line. Between these two positions lie the disputed waters. The fishermen from both countries see this disputed area as rich with their rightful fish. It falls to the Coast Guard to enforce this boundary disputed area. The fact that the two nations can't agree on the correct line of demarcation makes for the possibility of a politically sensitive incident with international consequences. As an instrument of national policy the Service flies patrols by helicopters from Sitka and has a patrol boat either on scene or available to respond at a moments notice. Seizures of violators are common. While no shots had been fired in anger on my watch, the threat of violence was common. While I was Chief of Search and Rescue and the Program Managers for Alaskan patrol boats and air stations, I dreaded an incident in which someone was killed over disputed fish. The world is dangerous enough without having to create conflicts with one of our closest allies who helped us defend Alaska during World War II. Canadian blood was also shed in retaking two occupied Aleutian Islands in 1946.[6]

6   PA1 Mike Milliken, "Canadian Fishermen Caught Crossing the Line", (Juneau, *The Alaska Bear*, Jul-Sep 1991) 4-7

Chapter Seven

Defense Readiness

The Revenue Cutter Service, and the Coast Guard that followed, has been a military Service from its creation. For over 220 years the Coast Guard has served the nation as one of the five armed forces. Throughout its history the Service has enjoyed a unique relationship with the Navy. By statute, the Coast Guard is an armed force, operating in the joint arena at any time and functioning as a specialized service under the Navy in time of war or when directed by the President. The Coast Guard also has command responsibilities for the U.S. Maritime Defense Zone, countering potential threats to America's coasts, ports and inland waterways through numerous port-security, harbor-defense and coastal-warfare operations and exercises. [1]

A Defense Readiness Story, Maritime Defense Zone Alaska
My primary specialty in the Coast Guard was aviation. My secondary track was military readiness based on the fact that I had attended the Armed Forces Staff College (AFSC) in Norfolk Virginia. AFSC had its name changed since I attended to the Joint Forces Staff College. The function of the school is the same, to get individual service members to think jointly and to become more familiar with each service's distinct way of operating. Eisenhower saw that lack of standardization and willingness to cooperate was

---

1 USCG Fact File, *National Security,* (Headquarters G-CP, 11/5/2006)

a problem when he was the leader of the allied forces for D-Day. Accordingly, the AFSC was created in 1946.

Armed Forces Staff College
I attended the AFSC from January to June 1976. This was a unique opportunity. We were divided into seminars of eighteen officers. Each seminar had six Navy, six Army and six Air Force midgrade officers. We also had three faculty advisors, one from each service. The unofficial motto was "Think Purple." Purple was the color of "jointness" as opposed to entrenched and divided individual service cultures (blue suiters, green suiters, etc.). In each seminar one quota was taken by a civilian DOD or other governmental agency employee. In our case we had a CIA map intelligence expert who took one of the air force quotas. There was also a foreign officer in each seminar. My seminar had a German Army artillery officer. Finally there was a Marine in each group in one of the six Navy positions. The Coast Guard was allowed two attendees of the 324 total. I took a Navy slot in our seminar also. This was the best-run organization with which I've ever been associated. This was an accompanied tour meaning that everyone brought his or her families. The administration managed to get all 324 families into fully equipped quarters, with schools for the children and family activities all arranged in a two-day period. We were there for six months, and it was an enlightening experience.

Each day in the seminar began with different members presenting topics that they were assigned to research. Each afternoon we had top-level briefings from service chiefs, academy superintendents, major commands and senior officials. General Alexander Haig who was Commander-in-Chief Europe at the time was particularly impressive to me. He walked into the center of the stage and just started talking for 30 minutes extemporaneously. However, the Coast Guard presented nothing in the six months. This was despite that fact that the Fifth CG District Headquarters Admiral's office was only a few miles away. The Armed Forces Staff College forgot one of its own armed forces.

Readiness Assignments

The AFSC experience led to three assignments in the Readiness area during my thirty-year career. The last was from 1988 to 1993. This was my last five years of active duty, and I was assigned as the Chief of Readiness for the Coast Guard in Alaska planning for problems, be they natural or man made. War-plans were devised and exercised to test them.

Included in the job was contingency planning for the Service on the last frontier. This meant developing plans not only for natural disasters, like tsunamis, floods and the like, but military contingencies as well. During this time we were still in a Cold War and the Soviet Union was only a short distance across the Bering Straits. This is not to say that the Coast Guard had the expertise, equipment or élan to defend against a major attack then or now. That was for the big brothers in the Defense Department to handle. Our portion of guarding Alaska was planning for port security and safety, terrorist threats to the maritime infrastructure, and the safe operation of commercial vessels in Alaska waters. This sounds a lot like Homeland Security but we didn't yet have that nomenclature in our vocabulary.

Naval Component of the Alaskan Command

The defense of Alaska is assigned to the Alaska Command, which is a sub-unified command under the Pacific Command in Hawaii. The original Alaska Command was established on 1 January 1947 based on lessons learned in WWII when the lack of unity of command hampered the Aleutian campaign. The Navy's Alaskan Sea Frontier headquartered at Kodiak was the naval component. Following the drawdown after the Vietnam War, the Alaskan Sea Frontier was disestablished, and the large Kodiak base became the responsibility of the Coast Guard. With no naval component, the planning for the defense of the Aleutians reverted back to the Pacific Command in Hawaii. This was despite Senator Ted Stevens' declaration that he didn't want any "Hawaiian pineapple admiral" making decisions about Alaska. Once again there was no unity of command in Alaska. This was to be addressed as part of the largest peacetime exercise since World War II, known as Pacific Exercise or PACEX.

During my tour as D17 Chief of Readiness, the head of Joint Task Force Alaska was Lieutenant General Tom McInerney, USAF who was the commander of the Alaskan Air Command. McInerney was invited to play PACEX as the Alaskan Command Commander. This was even though there was no "Alaskan Command" authorized. He, in turn, approached the Coast Guard District Commander, Rear Admiral (RADM) Ed Nelson and invited him to participate in the exercise as the naval component. Accomplished in 1988, PACEX involved two carrier battle groups transiting through the Aleutians. The Cold War was still relatively hot, and Alaska played a significant role.

As the head of the Coast Guard in Alaska, RADM Nelson also wore a Navy hat as the Alaska Maritime Defense Zone Commander. Nelson was one of my favorite bosses. He was in the class of 1953 from the Academy, and had been my commanding officer at CG Air Station Kodiak. The Admiral had also attended the Armed Forces Staff College, as had I. He had previously been the Superintendent of the Coast Guard Academy and was wearing the title of "Ancient Albatross" as the longest designated Coast Guard aviator on active duty.

RADM Nelson in Ancient Albatros uniform

PACEX
Lieutenant General Tom McInerney had been invited to come to Pacific Command Headquarters in Hawaii to plan for and exercise PACEX. He was going to play not as Joint Task force Alaska but as Commander Alaskan Command, a sub-unified command under the Pacific Command (PACOM). This was significant politically. McInerney invited Nelson to come with him to be his naval component. The admiral in turn invited me to come as his staff. During the exercise, only the principles were in the main room, (which we staff wienies called the Elephant Room). The bosses of every major military command in the Pacific were there and playing. I had never seen so many stars assembled in my life. The elephants would map out their strategy in the morning and then we staffers would "make it happen". This meant working out the logistics, orders, and movements. It was heady stuff but we held our own. The Alaskan Command was reactivated on 7 July 1989 with the new D17 Commander Rear Admiral David Ciancaglini on the dais as the naval component commander.

Defining the National Defense Mission of the Coast Guard
Because of our new "joint-ness" I frequently gave briefings about what the Coast Guard did or didn't do in Alaska. My audiences were often senior members of other U. S. armed services. You would think that if anyone would know what the Coast Guard does these senior officials would; more often they did not. Part of the problem was that they didn't understand how the Coast Guard was wearing a Navy hat. An explanation of maritime defense zones was necessary

Despite its name, the Coast Guard is not charged with defending the U. S. coastline, the Navy is. Up until the mid-1970's, the Navy had a command structure known as the Naval Sea Frontier that was responsible for planning the coastal defense of the United States. In my experience, the Navy appeared to be more interested in power projection and coastal defense planning took a very low priority. Enter the Coast Guard.

Maritime Defense

On 7 March 1984 the Secretary of the Navy and the Secretary of Transportation, who was the Coast Guard's boss at the time, signed a Memorandum of Agreement that specified the Coast Guard Area Commanders in the Atlantic and Pacific were given additional collateral duties as Commander, Maritime Defense Zone Atlantic, and Commander, Maritime Defense Zone Pacific. As such they reported to the respective navy fleet commanders. Commander, Maritime Defense Zone Atlantic, and Commander, Maritime Defense Zone Pacific responsibilities were to plan for the defense of the United States coastal zones including the ports and infrastructure. The responsibility was broken down further into sectors. Alaska got two sectors; the Alaskan Sector, and the Aleutian Sectors. A rear admiral headed each sector. The Seventeenth Coast Guard District Commander got the additional hat of Commander, Maritime Defense Zone, Alaska. A Navy reserve rear admiral was Commander, Maritime Defense Zone Aleutians. This is how we got the Navy hat. The term "hat" refers to the uniform head covering worn which represents the Service of that "hat." Wearing a "Navy hat" means being in the Navy "Chain of Command."

Navy and Coast Guard Reserve units from outside Alaska augmented both sectors. This was a monumental responsibility in planning, training, and coordination. Fortunately the Cold War thawed before we needed to actually try out our plans for real. Maritime Defense Zone has basically been shelved for now although its structure fits well into the Homeland Security model. The responsibility for protection of our ports and harbors is back with the Coast Guard. Since 9/11 and with the formation of the Department of Homeland Security this is even more of a priority. As with all Coast Guard missions, any operational unit can be assigned defense tasking, given the threat. The mission of port and coastal security is now the number one mission of the Coast Guard as far as budgetary spending.

Why is the Coast Guard Involved With Defense Readiness?

When in 1790 Congress authorized the building of the first ten boats establishing a "fleet of cutters" at the request of Treasury Secretary Alexander Hamilton, the primary function of these small boats was to enforce the customs laws. In 1799 Congress provided that the President could place the cutters under the orders of the Secretary of the Navy. When the Quasi war with France broke out one year later, the one-year-old Navy had no ships. The Revenue Cutters were the entire fleet the nation had to defend its waters. During the conflict France seized 340 U. S. ships.[2]

On, 4 August 1949, the Coast Guard's 154th birthday, a Congressional act specified that the Coast Guard "shall be a military service and a branch of the armed forces of the United States at all times."[3] Congress was completing the paperwork as it were, as the Service had been transferred into the Navy in 1940 prior to the declaration of war.

Similarly, the Service, fresh from its 1915 consolidation with the Lifesaving Services was transferred into the Navy for WWI. In fact the Revenue Cutter Service, and later the U. S. Coast Guard, has fought in every armed conflict of our nation. The Service has the distinction of firing the first naval shot of the Civil War when the cutter *Harriet Lane,* at Charleston Harbor, fired a warning shot across the bow of the steamer *Nashville* during the confederate shelling of Fort Sumter. Another fateful distinction is the fact that when the Cutter *Tampa* was torpedoed in WWI with the loss of all 115 hands on a convoy mission; it resulted in the Coast Guard having the highest percentage of casualties of any U.S. Armed Service in that entire war.

President Clinton said

> "The threat to our national security today comes
> not from those who control enemy missile silos
> but from the international criminals and drug

---

2   *USCG Missions Timeline,* "National Security"

3   United States Code, Title 14, Part One, Chapter One, Article One

traffickers who undermine the stability of fragile new democracies and threaten the future of our children. Coast Guard men and women are poised to meet these new challenges and their work is vital to helping secure a better future for America."[4]

Defense Readiness in Alaska

Alaska once again shows its uniqueness as the military tasking for the Coast Guard there is unlike anywhere else. To my knowledge, the Coast Guard in Alaska is the only place that the Service is designated as the naval component of a Department of Defense joint command, the Alaskan Command.

Alaska Command Staff participating in PACEX; LTGEN McInerney is 4th from left, RADM Nelson on his left the author on far right front row

---

4   National Security and the U. S. Coast Guard (COMDT PUB 16011.1) April 1997

Following PACEX, we accomplished some horse-trading with the Navy, and ten naval billets were established in the Coast Guard staff in Juneau. As I was retired when the Department of Homeland Security was formed, I have had no personal experience with it. I can say that the relocation of the Coast Guard into a new agency with twenty-two separate components presented some organizational restructuring, i.e. turf battles. The personality of the Service has changed. I'm not qualified to say whether it's good or bad. It's ironic, however, that the readiness mission with which I spent much of my time after my operational flying was over has all of a sudden become much more of a priority than when I was involved. I never even had a set of battle dress uniform (BDU'S), the standard work uniform for the modern Coast Guard.

Chapter Eight

Marine Environmental Protection

Marine Environmental Protection (MEP) became a mission in 1822 when the *Timber Reserve Act* was passed, which required the Revenue Cutter service to protect the Oak trees required in ships construction.[1] When I was flying H-3's in Kodiak, MEP was one of the most frequently used codes for the operational flights. We would routinely check Cook Inlet's oil platforms as well the many harbors around the island. We were also involved with the construction of the Marine Safety office Valdez Vessel Traffic System by transporting the radar dishes to the remote sites by helicopter. Little did we know back in 1975 the gigantic mess the Coast Guard would be involved with thirteen years later with the *Exxon Valdez*.

A Marine Environmental Story - The T/V *Exxon Valdez* Grounding

I was sitting in the Chief of Staff's office waiting for a decision that could change my career. Captain Dave Worth was, in effect, acting Alaska Coast Guard District Commander, as Admiral Nelson was totally occupied in Valdez with the oily nightmare

---

1   *USCG Missions Timeline.* Environmental Protection/Scientific Efforts, 11

that was the *Exxon Valdez* spill. Up to this time I had been largely unaffected by the environmental disaster, but that was about to change. Nelson needed a relief as his deputy Federal On Scene Coordinator (FOSC), and he had nominated me.

The problem was that a major Maritime Defense Zone (MDZ) conference was to be held in San Diego in the near future. As I explained earlier, MDZ was my program as Chief of Readiness. One of the many hats that Admiral Nelson wore was one as MDZ Sector Alaska Commander. My staff and I managed that program for him and dealt with the other military in Alaska as well as our Navy and Coast Guard Reserve units.

With Nelson unable to leave Valdez, the Coast Guard Pacific Area headquarters was adamant that I needed to attend the conference of all the Pacific area sectors to present the Alaska perspective. The senior man won, the three star in Pacific Area, and I went to San Diego and not Valdez. I thus, thankfully, missed a chance to be part of Alaskan history.

The grounding and oil spill of the *Exxon Valdez* is another of the defining events in the history of Alaska. It ranks with World War II and the Good Friday 1964 earthquake in the impact it had on the collective psyche of Alaskans. The ramifications of the spill, its impact on the environment, the Alaskan residents and the legal trials that followed took twenty years to only partially resolve. How did the Coast Guard get involved in this scenario? The simple answer is that its part of our job.

The Mess Begins

Each working day at 0900 in the Coast Guard District office in Juneau, the division chiefs would gather in the Operation Center with the District Commander, in this case RADM Edward Nelson. The Admiral was a role model to me as I said earlier. He also loved Alaska and came back whenever he could. So did I.

Present this Friday morning briefing, in addition to the duty controller and the Operations Center duty staff, was the Chief of Search and Rescue (OSR) my old friend Capt. Mike Stenger and the Division Chiefs, primarily Captains, in charge of Operations

(O), Carl Luck, myself, as Chief of Readiness (R), and the Chief of Marine Safety (M) Captain Glenn Haines.

Admiral Nelson and the rest of us gathered around the chart of Prince William Sound to have Glenn explain what had happened. All we knew was that we had before us a profoundly serious situation. I don't think any of us expected it to turn into the nightmare that it became for the nation, the State of Alaska, and the Coast Guard. It was Friday 24 March 1989 (Good Friday). This was also the 25th anniversary of the 8.6 earthquake that reformatted Alaska. Haines said, "Admiral, this one is big." Glenn was speaking of the tanker, *Exxon Valdez* running aground shortly after midnight that night. At the time we had no concept how big and how much of all our time would be dedicated to the cleanup and its aftermath.

Up to this time operation of the trans-Alaska pipeline (TAPS) and the port of Valdez had been tremendously successful. As of 1988 over 6.6 billion barrels of oil flowed through and out of the pipeline and the terminal.[2] The current flow represented about seventeen percent of total U. S. oil production.[3] The operation of the terminal at Valdez was under the supervision of Alyeska Pipeline Service Co.[4] All this success came crashing down in the early morning hours of Good Friday 1989. As this was a very controversial event, I want to review the facts.

---

2   Cohen, *Alaska Pipeline*, unnumbered back page

3   Alaska Almanac, 31st Edition, 171

4   Cohen, *Alaska Pipeline*, 137.

Exxon Valdez

The Players

The giant tanker, The T/V *Exxon Valdez* (E/V), and its Captain, Joe Hazelwood, were both to go down in infamy. This was incongruent with the history of both up to this point. The subsequent disaster involving the two was to be characterized by Brian O'Neill, the attorney for the plaintiffs, as the greatest drunk driving accident in history.[5] The *Exxon Valdez* was delivered to its owner on 11 December 1986. The vessel's dimension were 987 feet length overall, width of 166 feet, and with a fully loaded draft of 64.5 feet.[6] Her construction was single hull with a single five bladed propeller driven by an eight-cylinder, slow speed, Sulzer reversible marine diesel engine rated at 31,610 brake horsepower. The *Exxon Valdez* maximum continuous cruising speed was 16.25 knots. This behemoth had but one function, to economically transport crude oil products. When fully loaded, she could carry 1.48 million barrels of crude in her nine cargo tanks.

In charge of this giant oil tank was Joe Hazelwood. Hazelwood up to this time was regarded as one of Exxon's top ship drivers. He

5   Lebedoff, *Cleaning Up*, 138

6   Skinner and. Reilly, *The Exxon Valdez Oil Spill*, 3

was 42 years of age and had been with Exxon Shipping Company for twenty-one years, half his life. He had been hired as a third mate in June of 1968 following graduation from the State University of New York Maritime College with a BS in Marine Transportation. He was very intelligent having an IQ tested at 138 in high school. He earned his Masters license when he was thirty-two years of age, and at the time was the youngest captain in the Exxon fleet. He had a reputation for seamanship and the ability to handle danger. He also had a reputation of being a problem drinker.

His driver's license had been suspended or revoked three times by the state of New York for alcohol violations. At the time of the *Exxon Valdez* grounding his New York driving privileges had been suspended for a DUI in September of 1988. In April of 1985 he had voluntarily admitted himself for a twenty-eight day rehabilitation program at South Oakes Hospital in Amityville, New York. Following his release he had been granted ninety days leave to attend Alcoholics Anonymous. If he did, the twelve-step program obviously didn't impact his illness positively.[7]

Valdez Oil Terminal

---

7   Lebedoff, *Cleaning Up*, 7

The Exxon Valdez Arrives

The *Exxon Valdez* had moored at the Valdez terminal at 2300 on 22 October 1989. During the next day Joe did some errands. He ordered flowers for his daughter, he visited a number of people he knew in different offices and he had some drinks. Hazelwood went to the Pipeline Club, a favorite watering hole in Valdez, around 1700 with the ship's chief engineer. At his subsequent trial he admitted to having three vodkas. At the same trial, the lawyer for the prosecution pointed out that the bartenders at the Channel Club were very generous with their pours and one drink was really a double, the equivalent of two drinks.[8] Exxon had a rule that prohibited drinking four hours before sailing. The problem with that rule was that there was no enforcement on the captain and this captain obviously needed to be closely supervised.

The Accident

The *Exxon Valdez* cast off its mooring lines at 2112 on 23 March for its twenty-fourth voyage from the Valdez terminal with a load of fifty-three million gallons of crude oil. Her draft was approximately fifty-five feet with this load.

Prior to casting off, the *Exxon Valdez* had taken on a ship's pilot, Captain Murphy. Pilots are geographical experts for their assigned ports and they actually control the vessel during transit. The Captain of the vessel however is always responsible for the safe operation of his ship. The Valdez pilots were taken off the departing tankers once entering the open Prince William Sound. The reasons for not having them stay on for the entire transit to Hinchinbrook Entrance where the open ocean began were several. There was the practical danger of the pilots disembarking by rope ladder to a small pilot boat in the ocean swells, the expense, and the false sense of security twelve years of safe tanker transits had bred. Murphy stated at the subsequent investigation that he had smelled alcohol on Hazelwood's breath, but they were old acquaintances and said nothing about it at the time.

---

8   ibid, 10

Shortly after departing, with Murphy conning the vessel, Hazelwood left the bridge and went below. The pilot thought this was unusual, and against Exxon Company rules, but said nothing to Hazelwood.[9] The ship continued down the narrows to Rocky Point, approximately fourteen miles from the terminal where the pilots normally departed. Murphy ordered Hazelwood to report to the bridge so he could depart via the rope ladder to the pilot boat. At approximately 2324 Hazelwood called VTS Valdez and reported the pilot departing. The sole radar operator at Marine Safety Office/Vessel Traffic System Valdez was a civilian employee of the Coast Guard, Gordon Taylor.

Setting Up For An Accident
Hazelwood radioed that he would be adjusting the ship heading to port (left) into the inbound lane to avoid ice chunks coming from the Columbia Glacier. Most of this ice was not big enough to cause a problem to a tanker, however the occasional house sized pieces, known as growlers, were a risk. Taylor acknowledged the report, and said the inbound lane had no traffic and the nearest inbound tanker had not reached Hinchinbrook Entrance. Hazelwood gave the command to the helmsman to come left to a course of 200 degrees and ten minutes later, to 180 degrees, which would cause the vessel to depart from the outbound channel and cut across the 2,000-yard wide separation zone and the 1,500-yard inbound-channel. Hazelwood also engaged the autopilot, which would bring the vessel up to cruising speed. Third Mate Cousins was also on the bridge. Hazelwood briefed him of the situation and told him he was going below to his cabin to do some paperwork. Hazelwood told Cousins to return to the outbound course by turning abeam Busby light, which they could see ahead. The captain then left the bridge.

Ten minutes before midnight, the helmsman was changed, with Robert Kagen, only recently promoted to able seaman, taking over the helm. Cousins, wanting to make sure of turning at the proper point, left the bridge for the chart house to make some

---

9   ibid, 13

calculations. Kagen was left alone on the bridge. While Cousins and Hazelwood both did their respective paperwork, the giant tanker was steadily steaming towards the rocks of Bligh Reef.[10]

The first person to successfully do her job was the lookout Maureen Jones. She rushed into the bridge to give the first warning of disaster when she observed that the red buoy on Bligh Reef was on the wrong side of the ship. Every seaman knows that red buoys are taken on the right or starboard hand returning to port, "Red Right Returning." In this case the flashing red buoy which should have been to the left or port side, was to starboard. She voiced her concern to Cousins.[11] He first gave a ten-degree rudder command to starboard to the helmsman. It was unclear in the Coast Guard investigation that followed, or in the subsequent trial, whether the helmsman disengaged the autopilot. At any rate the ship failed to respond. At this speed it would take nearly 6/10th of a mile for the ship to turn. Cousins next ordered twenty degrees rudder, then finally hard right rudder. He called Hazelwood on the ship's telephone reporting, "I think we are in serious trouble." At approximately the same time the ship shuddered as if it was going over a speed bump. The time was 0004, four minutes past midnight on Friday 24 March 1989.[12]

Hard Aground

Hazelwood raced to the bridge. The smell of oil was overpowering. He shined searchlights on the water and could see oil coming up in geysers on both sides of the vessel. His next actions likely compounded the problem. For the next fifteen minutes he kept the engines going full ahead as he moved the rudder from hard right to hard left. The ship swung slightly, probably opening the ship even more. The Chief Mate Kunkel, fearing that the ship might capsize, rushed to the bridge and calculated the vessel's stability. At the time the ship was listing four to five degrees to starboard. Kunkel told Hazelwood that the ship was too unstable

---

10   ibid, 15

11   ibid, 15

12   Skinner, 3

to move. However, the Captain continued his efforts. Finally, at 0027 Hazelwood called the VTS reporting themselves aground in his infamous statement that "we've fetched, run aground north of Goose Island around Bligh Reef."[13]

Vessel Traffic System Valdez

The watch stander at Vessel Traffic System operations was now Bruce Blansford. Taylor had briefed Blansford about the *Exxon Valdez* having diverted from the outbound track, however Blansford did not take any actions to track the vessel. The VTS was concerned primarily with the radar coverage in the restricted area from the terminal to the Valdez Narrows. Beyond the Narrows, the radar coverage was spotty. After setting up the room to his liking, Blansford went to the galley to get a cup of coffee.[14] The first he knew the *Exxon Valdez* was in danger was the call from Hazelwood. The Coast Guard would later be found at fault by various governmental investigations for not having sufficient radar coverage outside the narrows.

Blansford woke up his boss at home, Commander Steve McCall, the commanding officer of Marine Safety Office (MSO) Valdez at 0030. McCall raced to the traffic control center. He knew that this was the nightmare that all in command fear. In one of the many ironies of this tragedy, McCall, who was within three months of retiring, had been a classmate of Hazelwood's at the New York Maritime School. He raised the *Exxon Valdez* on the radio asking for a status report. Hazelwood reported that he did not have an update but that they were attempting to work off the reef. McCall cautioned Hazelwood to take it slow and easy, to not do any "ripping" and that they had about another hour and a half of rising tide in their favor.[15]

Hazelwood radioed back that he felt the major damage had been done, that they had "kind of…rolled over it and were hung up by the stern." At the time of the grounding the *Exxon Valdez*

---

13   Davidson, 19

14   Lebedoff, 145

15   Davidson 19

had a loaded draft of fifty-six feet. The charted depth where she ran aground was thirty feet at low tide.[16] With a high tide in the area of approximately twelve feet it meant that she had ripped through approximately sixteen feet of Alaskan rock. Subsequent investigation by divers over the next two weeks would show that a total of eleven tanks out of fifteen had been opened to the sea. Some of these tanks were for ballast and held no oil.

Spill Contingency Plans

There were six spill contingency plans in place including the National Contingency Plan to site-specific plans for Prince William Sound. The operating company for the Valdez Terminal, Alyeska, had its plan. MSO Valdez had its plan, and the Alaska State Oil and Hazardous Substances Pollution Contingency Plan outlined the state's role.[17]

All of these plans identified a Federal On Scene Coordinator (FOSC). This heavy load fell on the shoulders of the U. S. Coast Guard Captain of the Port Valdez, Commander Steve McCall.

Day One of the Response and Clean-up
Responders on Scene

Meanwhile the first three responders had made it to the *Exxon Valdez* by way of the *Silver Bullet*, the high-speed pilot boat. At 0345 Lieutenant Commander Thomas Falkenstein of MSO, Chief Warrant Officer Mark Delozier and Dan Lawn, Alaska Department of Environmental Conservation (DEC) came to the bridge.[18] Falkenstein determined that 138,000 barrels had already been lost and that the ship was losing an additional 20,000 barrels an hour. He subsequently radioed Commander McCall and told him that the *Exxon Valdez* was in danger of breaking apart on the rocks or capsizing.[19] McCall in turn called Alyeska and said the priority should be to make arrangements

16   Skinner, 3

17   ibid, 5

18   Lebedoff, 38

19   Davidson, 22

to remove the oil from the *Exxon Valdez* to another tanker to prevent its entire load from being lost.[20] As there was only the one tug and barge available, the Alyeska crew began locating the equipment for lightering (removal of cargo) including six-inch diameter hose and large fenders. To make room, the boom and equipment that had been previously loaded onto the barge was offloaded. Again more time was lost.

Blood Sample Chain of Custody
On board the *Exxon Valdez* Falkenstein and Delozier smelled alcohol on the breath of Hazelwood. They called the MSO requesting that someone be sent out to take blood samples. Finally around 0600 a second boat arrived with an Alaska State Trooper. There had been a miscommunication however, and the Trooper thought he had been requested to quell an unruly person and he had no testing equipment. Finally a small two-seater helicopter showed up with a Coast Guard Hospital Corpsman on board equipped with blood sampling supplies. He took samples from Hazelwood, Brothers, the helmsman Kagen, and the lookout Jones. The samples were taken nearly eleven hours after the grounding.[21]

When the corpsman returned to MSO Valdez he found that the keys for the urinalysis sample refrigerator were on the person of a petty officer out on a boat enforcing the security zone around the *Exxon Valdez*. In what he thought was a good idea at the time he took the blood samples to the galley and put them in the big walk-in refrigerator. Unfortunately the refrigerator was left unlocked that night and the positive chain-of-custody required for the samples was broken. This would have a major impact on the subsequent trial.

The MSO personnel on the *Exxon Valdez* interviewed Hazelwood on the bridge. Despite the heavy volatile fumes, Hazelwood was smoking a cigarette, which Delozier asked him to put out. At 0530 the spill was estimated to be 240,000 barrels.

---

20   ibid, 23

21   Lebedoff, 40

An earlier helicopter flight at 0730 had estimated the area of the slick as 1,000 feet wide and four miles long. It was obvious from the start that the response equipment on hand at Alyeska was stupendously inadequate.[22]

The U. S. Coast Guard Pacific Area Strike Team at the inactive Hamilton AFB north of San Francisco was notified and requested to assist.[23] These USCG strike teams, on the West, East and Gulf Coast are trained to respond to pollution incidents anywhere in the world 24/7 and have special air deployable equipment for such tasks as lightering a vessel. The tanker *Exxon Baton Rouge* was contacted at 0414 and told to proceed to the position of the *Exxon Valdez* in order to offload the cargo from the stricken vessel. She arrived at the grounding at 2010 and was moored port side to port side along side the *Exxon Valdez*.

Alaska Governor Cowper and Staff On Scene
At 1700 Alaska Governor Steve Cowper and key staff members including the Commissioner of DEC Dennis Kelso flew to the site of the grounding by floatplane and were taken to the *Exxon Valdez* by Coast Guard small boat. They saw very little going on as the skimmers were by now full with no place to discharge the oil. The amount of booms was less than twenty percent of what would be needed to surround a four-mile long slick. A Coast Guard Marine Safety officer who also was on scene told me later the oil was so thick that if a candy bar were thrown onto the oil it would sit as if it was on the ground.

Exxon On Scene Commander
Exxon's big gun for the cleanup was Frank Iarossi. He had been the President of Exxon Shipping since 1982. This was no small operation with eighteen tug and barges, and nineteen ocean going tankers. In a not unfamiliar coincidence, Iarossi was a 1959 graduate of the Coast Guard Academy. Frank had served ten years in the Coast Guard before he left to go into private consulting

22   Davidson, 28

23   Skinner, Appendices-1

business. During his time in the Coast Guard, he had earned master's degrees in mechanical engineering and naval architecture. After leaving the CG he also earned an MBA. He interviewed with Exxon after learning that they were seeking engineers saying at the time it was just for the interview experience. Exxon made the experience a good one by offering him the job.[24]

Dispersant Controversy

The use of dispersants became a very controversial issue between the three key players: The Federal On Scene Coordinator, the State, and Exxon.[25] In charge of enforcing the State's position was Dennis Kelso, Commissioner of DEC. At 41, Kelso had been in his job for two years. His background included undergraduate training in science and a law degree from Harvard. The State had oversight of the Alyeska operation and DEC had that responsibility. There were many aspects of the state's economy that were involved with the situation. Royalties from the oil industry were funding nearly ninety percent of the state government unrestricted revenue.[26] Prince William Sound was also a critical area for commercial fisheries. Adding even more complications, it was an important historical area rich in Native Alaskan heritage sites. The state had pre-approved the use of dispersants in the offshore areas. In-shore was another matter.

Day Two, 25 March

Saturday, 25 March, the second day, began well. The tug *Jeffrey Foss* had arrived shortly after midnight with a 30,000-barrel capacity barge to permit the skimmers to off load. At 0736 the oil transfer began from the *Exxon Valdez* to the *Baton Rouge*. After an hour the transfer using the *Exxon Valdez* pumps and piping was halted due to piping damage. The external pumps brought to the scene were thereafter used to transfer the oil. At 0750 the divers completed their first underwater examination of the *Exxon*

---

24   ibid, 30

25   Skinner, 17

26   *Alaska Almanac* 31st edition, 168

Valdez. The news was not good. Holes were found in eleven tanks. The vessel designer advised the Coast Guard that the ship was not floatable and that a major salvage operation would be required.[27]

Day Three, 26 March
On Sunday, 26 March, day three, the Pacific Area Strike Team came aboard the *Exxon Valdez* at 0530 to assist with the transfer of oil. By now Exxon had contracted with over 100 people to begin clean up. A number of fishing boats were also contracted at inflated prices. This quickly spawned the phrase "spillionaire" signifying someone who was going to make a lot of money doing the clean up.

After several delays, at 1600, a C-130 air deployment of dispersant test was completed with good results. The plan was to start doing the spraying in earnest the next day. As often happens in Alaska, Mother Nature had other plans and during the night the good weather disappeared. Winds nearing 70 knots developed with rough seas associated with them. The spill, which had been somewhat cooperative, quickly began to move, spread out and threaten very sensitive fish hatcheries.

Day Four, 27 March
By 1900 Monday, 27 March, 124,000 barrels of oil had been transferred to the *Baton Rouge.* This was only about twelve percent of the *Exxon Valdez* cargo and the clock was ticking.[28]

The Media Circus
Over the weekend, the *Exxon Valdez* spill had obtained epic news proportions. By Sunday there were more media people than cleanup personnel. General admission news conferences, morning and evening, were held.[29] These quickly became the best show in town as the frustrations of the local fishermen began to reach a boiling point. Much of their anger was directed at Exxon and its desire to

---

27   Skinner, Appendices-3

28   ibid, Appendices-6

29   Skinner, 22

use dispersants. The fisherman felt that this would permanently damage the already damaged ecosystem. While the debate went on for several days, on the third day the weather turned Alaskan. High winds generated 20-foot waves in Prince William Sound. Boats could not leave the harbor and planes were grounded.

The Director of my local Jefferson County Department of Emergency Management has a sign in his office "When the VIPs arrive, all progress stops." This was especially true with the E/V spill. Everyone needed to get his or her "environmental concern" ticket punched.

Captain Jay Crowe was Deputy Federal On Scene Commander, having been selected for the job that I nearly had were it not for the MARDEZ conference. Jay told me years later that the worst case was when Vice President Quayle visited and directed that all the CG District Commanders should come witness the operation. Getting to Valdez was never easy and especially so with all the turmoil going on. Nevertheless each Admiral had to make the pilgrimage and worse still, the busy staff of the cleanup had to make the preparation for the care and feeding of the visitors.

The Alaskan Command and the Spill

Fortunately The Alaska Command in Elmendorf Air Force Base with their greater resources and state of the art equipment took much of the VIP briefing load off the Valdez staff. LTGEN McInerney was a great believer in technology, and his staff had developed a very sophisticated 120 Apple computer based visual network called the Alaskan Command and Control Military Automated Network (ACCMAN), which soon became known as AXMAN. In order to assist, the ACCMAN system was converted to monitor the spill recovery efforts and became known as the Oil Spill Computer Aided Response (OSCAR), which was of great utility to FOSC and in briefing VIPs.

McInerney, and his Chief of Staff COL Tom Wilson US Army, were very supportive of the CG efforts in coordinating the complex multi-agency, civilian, fisherman and media demands. Tom was class of '63 from West Point, my year group at the USCG Academy, and we called each other classmates. He and I spoke frequently by phone about events going on to get a reality check from someone we could be frank with.

Alaskan Weather Blows In

With the increased winds, the slick, which had generally been localized, suddenly became a frothy beast of many tentacles, all heading southwest. The oil went ashore wherever it wanted. The smashing waves sent oil far above the high water mark. Too much oil, too little equipment, and too much Alaska weather now presented a complex cleanup that was to go on for three years. As this is written in 2011, twenty-three years after the spill, oil can still be found beneath the surface on many beaches, even though a major effort was made to clean up Prince William Sound.

Federal On Scene Commander Change

Vice Admiral Clyde Robbins, the Pacific Area Commander, had relieved Nelson in Valdez as Federal On Scene Commander on 15 April, at the direction of the Commandant ADM Yost. Rear Admiral Nelson returned to his normal District Commander duties.[30] In May, Robbins testified before the Committee on Interior and Insular Affairs. He stated that the Coast Guard had deployed seven major cutters, twenty aircraft, a variety of support vessels and over 1,000 personnel. Exxon had deployed approximately seventy miles of boom, fifty-five skimmers, 460 support vessels, and over 3,000 personnel.[31] Other federal response forces with the spill included: U. S. Navy twenty skimmers, ten tow boats, and ninety-four personnel; Forest Service thirty personnel and one helicopter; NOAA one helicopter, four Data Buoys and twenty-two personnel; FAA seven personnel; Dept. of Interior twenty-six personnel; EPA seven personnel; and National Guard ninety-three personnel.[32]

---

30   ibid, Appendices-16

31   Davidson, 186

32   Skinner, Appendices-20.

The cleanup efforts went on for three years. Rear Admiral David Ciancaglini, who became CG District Seventeen Commander upon Nelson's retirement, spent nearly all of his three-year assignment alternating between his Coast Guard duties in Juneau and his Federal On Scene Coordinator duties in Anchorage and Valdez. Ciancaglini was a tightly wound, detail type boss. I was sure that he was going to have a heart attack under the strain of the two jobs plus the Alaskan Command Naval Component duties. Fortunately he did not. The efforts were not without their critics. Many argued that much of what was done, including hot water, high pressure washing of the beaches did even more damage to the environment by killing the critical microorganisms. In the end Exxon spent nearly 2 billion dollars on the cleanup.

Lightering of the *Exxon Valdez*
One of the few bright spots in the *Exxon Valdez* saga was the successful lightering of the majority of the crude on the damaged behemoth. By Wednesday 29 March, day six, the *Exxon Baton Rouge* had successfully taken on 443 thousand barrels and departed. *Exxon San Francisco* took her place at 1100 on the 30th.[33] *Exxon San Francisco* completed her transfer reaching her capacity of 452,533 barrels and was in turn replaced by the *Exxon Baytown* to finish the transfer of oil.

---

33 Skinner, Appendicies-7

Oil being transferred from *Exxon Valdez* to *Exxon Baton Rouge*

Day Thirteen, 5 April

On 5 April, thirteenth day of the spill, *Exxon* Valdez was towed to Naked Island. After temporary repairs she was towed to a San Diego shipyard arriving on 10 June 1989. The repairs involved removing and replacing approximately 1,600 tons of steel at a cost of $30 million. Following repairs the vessel reentered service renamed the *Exxon Mediterranean*.[34]

---

34   Wikipedia, *Exxon Valdez*, Carrier, 1

The Exxon Valdez Trials
The legal story of the *Exxon Valdez* spill was equally complex, exasperating and interesting. There were really two different legal processes, one for the criminal charges and one for the damages.

The *Exxon Valdez* Criminal Trial
For the criminal charges, Hazelwood was acquitted of operating the tanker while drunk largely on the basis of the blood alcohol tests being disregarded due to the lack of positive control mentioned earlier. He was convicted of a misdemeanor offence of illegally discharging oil and was sentenced to 1,000 hours of community service cleaning up Anchorage highways.

The Punitive Trial
The punitive side of the case was decided on 16 September 1994 when a jury in the Anchorage Federal Court handed in a verdict of $5 billion against Exxon. This was the largest punitive settlement of its time.[35]

Exxon was not about to give up however. Exxon appealed this verdict several times with the damages being reduced to $2.5 billion by the 9th circuit court on one appeal. Finally it reached the Supreme Court where on 25 June 2008 the court reached a verdict saying that the punitive damages should not exceed $507.5 million.[36]

The process had been going on for nearly 20 years. Exxon had spent millions in legal fees but the interest alone on the original $5 billion settlement amount paid all its costs. The original jury reached the $5 billion amount using the logic that this was one year of Exxon's profits in 1988. Of the over 32,000 original plaintiffs, 3,000 had died before the settlement was reached. If there is any lesson to be learned, it is don't get complacent, practice the worst-case scenario, and pray it doesn't happen on your watch!

---

35   Lebedoff, 292

36   Wikipedia, *Exxon Valdez*

Why Does the Coast Guard do Marine Environmental Protection?

As big as the news was of the Exxon Valdez oil spill in Alaska, many no longer remember or maybe didn't know at the time that the Coast Guard was the overall federal agency in charge of the clean up. How in the world did the Coast Guard "Angels in Orange" get into this gooey political mess?

MEP Law

The law enforcement authority of the Coast Guard has very broad application. Perhaps none is more complicated than protection of the marine environment and the natural resources that are associated with it. The Service's responsibility goes back as far as 1822 when the *Timber Act* of that year tasked the Revenue Cutter Service with protecting government timber in Florida from poachers.[37] We saw earlier that the Revenue Cutter Service was charged with protecting seals in the Bering Sea from over harvesting even before this part of the world was under U. S. control. Water Quality enforcement has been a responsibility of the Coast Guard dating back to the *Refuse Act of 1899*. Major pieces of legislation that had far reaching application for the Service were the *Water Quality Improvement Act of 1970* and the *Federal Water Pollution Control Act of 1976*. Finally, a major piece of legislation that resulted from the Exxon Valdez spill was the *Oil Pollution Act of 1990* (OPA-90). Two of the many provisions of OPA-90 that affected the Coast Guard were the requirement to establish a fixed light structure on Bligh Reef within one year and to increase the coverage of the VTS system to track tanker vessels while within Prince William Sound and to have an alarm system to sound when vessels depart designated navigational routes.[38]

---

37   USCG Historian's Office, *USCG Missions Timeline*, Environmental Protection/Scientific Efforts, 11

38   Oil Pollution Act of 1990, Sec. 5003 Bligh Reef Lights, Sec 5004 Vessel Traffic Service System.

Marine Environmental Protection In Alaska

In the days I was flying helicopters out of Kodiak for various mission areas, we were frequently involved with environmental protection. From Kodiak Air Station we would regularly fly Cook Inlet to check on the sixteen oil and gas platforms there to ensure that they were not polluting Alaskan waters. We would also fly the perimeter of Kodiak Island to check on the villages and harbors, again looking for pollution. The management of the marine environmental program is the responsibility of the "M" guys. The Marine Environmental Program is divided geographically in Alaska between Marine Safety Office (MSO) Southeast (Juneau), MSO Western Alaska (Anchorage), and MSO Prince Williams Sound (Valdez). There are, or have been, marine safety detachments in Dutch Harbor, Sitka, Kenai, Ketchikan and Kodiak. The concept of marine safety is prevention. If that fails, the responsibility for managing the federal end of cleanup falls to the Marine Safety Offices.

Included in its responsibilities are marine environmental protection, investigation of maritime casualties, inspection and certification of vessels, commercial fishing industry vessel safety, licensing of personnel through the Regional Examination Centers in Anchorage and Juneau, port safety & security, recreational boating standards and control of the movement of dangerous cargoes. While the marine safety field is not glamorous, it is one of the most important missions in the Coast Guard. If prevention fails, however, the next mission of the Coast Guard takes over - Search and Rescue.

Chapter Nine

Search and Rescue (SAR).

Rescuing people in distress is the mission that propelled many of us to join the Coast Guard. Having personally saved over a hundred lives I can testify that it is the most rewarding mission of all.

A Rescue Story; The Fishing Vessel Manzanita

Like many memorable events in someone's life, this one began routinely. I was flying as co-pilot in one of the twin engine Sikorsky H-3 helicopter with LCDR Bob Ashworth, aircraft commander, out of Kodiak, Alaska. The date was 16 April 1975. Bob and I were doing a routine night training flight. We also had the duty, which meant we were the crew to respond if a request for assistance came up. All SAR air stations in the Coast Guard have a crew on duty 24/7. At this time in 1975 there were twenty-four air stations standing ready around the U.S., Hawaii and Puerto Rico.

To maintain qualifications pilots need to complete a certain number of events including hoists, water landings, night flying etc. every six months. Some of these events involved flying instrument approaches for landing in poor weather. This is what Bob and I were doing on that dark Kodiak night. I enjoyed flying with Bob. He had been two years ahead of me at the Academy and was a role model. We had been flying for about two hours when we were called by the duty officer to return to the base and switch aircraft for a boat aground in heavy surf 300 miles away by Cape St Elias. Switching aircraft would take less time than refueling the one we were flying.

The HH-3F Pelican

We rapidly changed aircraft and performed the necessary preflight on the fresh H-3. I loved and trusted this big truck of a helicopter. With its twin engines and sophisticated navigational systems it was a joy to fly. It also had a well-deserved reputation for being able to handle Alaska's challenges. Having over seven hours of endurance, and a boat hull for landing in the water, the rescue capabilities of this eleven-ton monster were considerable.

HH-3F 1496 on the ramp at Kodiak

After takeoff, we headed out across the Gulf of Alaska. The night was inky dark and snowing heavily. Flying at nearly 140 MPH the snow came at the windshield horizontally as if we were flying into a sky of cotton candy. I hoped that no seagulls were dumb enough to be flying in this stuff at our altitude because we would never see them in time to avoid a bird strike. The distance to the distress was over 300 miles and required going around Kayak Island where Cape St. Elias was located.

Cape St. Elias Lighthouse

Weather Conditions

En route we continued flying in constantly heavy snow, and the radar was not giving us a usable picture. The cabin crew consisted of the radio operator and the flight mechanic. The rescue swimmer program had not been started at this time. The crew and I, as copilot, were frequently checking the fuselage of the big helicopter for ice build up. Ice was a serious problem in that it added weight and reduced the aerodynamic efficiency of the rotor blades. To avoid this we flew as low as was safe. This was usually around 500 feet. Any lower than this meant that you would have little time to react to a problem such as loss of an engine. The prudent helicopter pilot always gave himself enough altitude to react in time to do a successful power off landing into the wind if possible. This maneuver is known as an autorotation.

I tuned in the radio beacon at Cape St. Elias at the seaward end of Kayak Island to insure we were going to fly around the island, which had some serious cliffs. The end of the island had shear rock walls over 500 feet, about the altitude we were flying.

The Distress: Vessel Aground in Surf

The duty controller at Kodiak had briefed us that we were looking for a brand new fishing vessel named the *Manzanita* with five crewmen aboard. It turned out that they were on their maiden trip to Alaska. What should have been a great trip had turned into a disaster when, being unfamiliar with the Alaskan waters, they had run aground on the shallow shore east of Kayak Island, and were being hammered by heavy surf.

After nearly three hours of flight, we safely flew around Kayak Island and headed in to try and pick up the shoreline visually. Despite the inky darkness and the snow, the crashing surf was visible below. Once over the breakers we started east in the surf line looking for the boat. Visibility was less than a mile in snow. The snow also made using any sort of a searchlight impractical. Bob had slowed the helicopter down to about 45 knots (52 MPH) because of the visibility restriction, but we still were over the boat before we could slow the big helicopter.

The Rescue

"Throw out a smoke" I directed Simms, the flight mechanic. The smoke float/flares are such that when they land in the water they actuate chemically, giving off a bright light for about thirty minutes. The bright flame gives the pilot a reference point in the turbulent seas. Bob did a 360-degree racetrack turn to seaward and came in over the boat descending to hoisting altitude. While in the turn we all completed our respective checklists for doing an over water hoist.

Once in a hover astern of the *Manzanita* we could see the waves were smashing against the boat and sending the frigid salt water nearly 50 feet in the air. Bob briefed the crew about the situation. Petty Officer Sims actuated the hydraulic hoist and when instructed, he went on "Hot Mike" to continually talk Ashworth over the hoisting area. This is a process that the pilots and crewmen practice frequently because once over the hoisting area the pilot can't see below the aircraft and so relies on the hoist operator to give him directions as well as to tell him what he is doing. Sims was calmly telling us what was happening as he lowered the rescue basket. Suddenly Sims said the fateful words "Oh shit." He began shouting that all five of the crew, who had been huddling behind the deckhouse, had grabbed onto the basket and would not let go. As the hoist was designed for only about 600 pounds there was no way to bring them up.

Although we were probably 300 yards off the sandy beach, Bob coolly said, "We'll drag them ashore." This is what we did. Sims kept talking to Bob as we dragged all five crew off the stricken vessel and slowly towed them to the beach. Despite the frigid waters, the survivors were so stressed that there was no way they were going to let go of their hold on the basket.

We nearly had our own accident in that I had not lowered the landing gear. The checklist for hoisting over water required leaving the landing gear retracted while over water. The decision to tow them ashore and the transition to the beach landing happened so fast that we didn't do the landing checklist again. Bob fortunately noticed it and yelled at me to lower the gear. The gear dropped just before we touched down on the stormy beach.

The five wet, cold, but happy survivors walked to the helicopter where they were given blankets and strapped in for the thirty-minute flight to the Cordova airport. At the airport an ambulance met us and took the cold and soggy sailors to the hospital. I never met any of the five that we saved that night. This was not unusual.

Of the hundred or so persons I saved over my 30 years flying, I only met a few face to face.

The *Manzanita* was on its first trip to Alaska, and it proved to be its last. Bob and I and the crew of the aircraft were all awarded CG Commendation Medals for the case. As challenging as this case was, it pales in comparison to one USCG Air Station Sitka handled a dozen years later.

A Special SAR Case; The Blue Bird

In the spring of 1988 I received orders to return to Alaska for a fourth tour, this time as Chief of Readiness. Readiness was a catchall for many diverse and unrelated programs. It included war plans, contingency planning, small arms training, maritime defense zone management, planning and running exercises and liaison with other services. This was important but it generally was not an important career enhancing assignment. This did not matter to me so much as it was getting me back to Alaska.

At the time I was working for Vice Admiral Jack Costello who as Commander Pacific Area was in charge of all Coast Guard operations on the west coast. When he retired in 1988 Vice-Admiral Clyde Robbins of Exxon Valdez FOSC fame in the previous chapter relieved him. At this time, Costello was still the boss in the Pacific and was going to Alaska, which was part of his area of responsibility, primarily to give a talk at the Propeller Club in Anchorage. He also had some other duties to perform. One was to participate in presenting awards to an aircrew at Sitka Air Station. This was not the usual SAR case, and I was very fortunate to be able to accompany him along with the District Commander, Rear Admiral Ed Nelson, my old boss, to Sitka to present the awards. All five crewmembers involved were to be awarded Distinguished Flying Crosses. Very rarely does this happen, but they deserved them. Here's the story.

The Distress: Vessel Sinking, Two POB

Four hours after sunset, on 10 December 1987 the air station at Sitka was notified of a distress call from the fishing vessel *Bluebird*, a twenty-six foot wooden fishing vessel that had struck a rock near St. Lazaria Island, about twenty miles from the air station. There were two persons on the *Bluebird*, Jim Blades and his six-year-old son, Clint.[1]

Blades had been out fishing commercially for winter king salmon and had anchored for the night when the weather became extremely bad, even for Alaska. Blades had acted prudently by seeking shelter from the ocean swells and high winds. Unfortunately the wind shifted and increased in strength, which was coupled with blinding snow. With the wind coming from a different direction and the danger of his anchor dragging in close proximity to the shoreline rocks, Blades had pulled up anchor to maneuver to open waters. The winds however increased in intensity, visibility dropped to near zero in blowing snow and Jim had lost his way. He suddenly came crashing down on a rock pinnacle, which holed his boat. He quickly transmitted a Mayday and told his son to don his survival suit while he attempted to put on his own.[2]

The Rescue Crew

Despite the extreme weather, Sitka Air Station launched the duty helicopter, the H-3 1486 with a crew of five. If there was any helicopter capable of handling these extreme conditions, it was the Sikorsky H-3. At over 11 tons, the twin engine H-3 was ruggedly built. The aircraft commander was Lieutenant Commander John Whiddon, copilot Lieutenant. G.B. Breithaupt, flight mechanic Aviation Machinist First Class Carl Saylor, radio operator Avionicsman Petty Officer Third Class Mark Milne and Rescue Swimmer Jeff Tunks. Whiddon was a very experienced Alaska pilot and, along with Carl Saylor, had been heroes of the *Prinsendam* rescue some seven years earlier. Both men had been nominated for the Distinguished Flying Cross for that historic case. He was on his fourth flying tour and was the engineering officer for Sitka. Despite this significant experience, John told me that these were the very worst conditions he experienced in his flying career.

---

1   Citation to Accompany the Award of the Distinguished Flying Cross to Jeffery D. Tunks Aviation Survivalman Second Class, USCG

2   Nancy Warren Ferrell, *Alaska's Heroes, A call to Courage*, 98

On Scene Conditions

Flight conditions were awful even by Alaskan standards. The wind was blowing hurricane force, with low ceilings and visibility greatly limited by blowing snow.

The site of the distress was less than twenty miles from the Sitka base, but it was close to high terrain, and the force of the winds and turbulence made progress slow and dangerous. Saint Lazaria is a national wildlife refuge at the base of the 3,200-foot high volcano, Mount Edgecombe. As occasionally happens with strong winds coming off high terrain like Edgecombe, the force of the wind can be amplified and made even more hazardous. An Alaskan term for this is Williwaw winds. The *Alaska Almanac* calls these winds the "bane of the mariner." Helicopter pilots are not fond of them either.

The 1486 crew encountered icing conditions crossing Sitka Sound and descended to three hundred feet of altitude. Icing is a double problem for helicopters in that in extreme cases if it forms on the rotating blades the aerodynamics change, which isn't good. If you can visualize a perfect airfoil becoming a baseball bat you can understand the problem.

"Where Are They?"

Arriving at the reported location, there was no sign of the little boat. Seas now were taller than a three-story house, which dwarfed the twenty-six foot boat. After searching in vain in the blowing snow and darkness and fighting the turbulent winds, the co-pilot Breithaupt directed Blades to count backwards from ten on his radio to allow the chopper to use their direction finding equipment to get a bearing on the boat. Proceeding along this line of bearing, the flight mechanic Saylor spotted a searchlight that Blades was alertly shining towards the helicopter.

The Rescue

Whiddon slugged his way over to the *Bluebird's* position. Progress was slow with the 60-knot headwinds. At times the gusts actually pushed the helicopter backwards. When they illuminated the boat with their searchlights they saw the situation was bad. The stern was underwater and the little boat was being tossed like a toy in the winds and thirty-foot seas. Suddenly the helicopter was hit by an extremely strong downdraft that pushed the bird down as if by a giant hand. In his left hand which controls the pitch on all the rotor blades, Whiddon pulled the collective up and up with little effect. They noted the torque at 122%, and they were still going back and down. Finally the nose high aircraft stopped with its tail rotor just a few feet above the violent seas. Slowly they climbed back up to hoisting altitude.

Hoisting directly from the *Bluebird* would be nearly impossible, as the wind would cause the basket to stream far behind the helicopter, and the boat was moving violently in the rough seas. Breithaupt radioed Blades that he and his son would have to enter the water for the rescue. Without hesitation Blades attached his young son's survival suit to his chest and jumped into the maelstrom. Conversing by phone with me, Whiddon explained that the son's survival suit was basically just a sort of mummy bag, and that Blades suit had no toggle on the zipper and he was unable to close it all the way. These suits are often called "Gumby Suits" after the little green cartoon character. The suit has totally enclosed mittens, which makes anything requiring manual dexterity nearly impossible. Without a toggle on the zipper the Gumby hands could not close the zipper. Consequently his suit soon filled with the icy water.[3]

"Swimmer Away"

At this early stage of the Coast Guard's Rescue Swimmer program, deployment of the swimmer was not done routinely and had never been done in conditions this extreme and dangerous.[4] Nevertheless when Whiddon asked his swimmer, Jeff Tunks, if he thought he could handle it, he answered affirmatively without hesitation. Tunks donned his mask and flippers and slid the rescue horse collar over his head and swung out the door. Saylor skillfully

---

3   ibid, 99

4   Laguardia-Kotite, Martha J, *So Others May Live*, 63

lowered Tunks while giving commands to the pilots who could not see the two survivors in the water. The violent winds once again pushed the helicopter back and Tunks entered the water almost a football field distance away from Jim Blades and his son. Tunks later said he could not find the father and son in the giant seas until the helicopter searchlight reflected off the reflective tape on their survival suits. With super-human effort, Tunks fought his way to the nearly exhausted and hypothermic father and son.

It took several passes in the hurricane force winds to place the basket where Tunks could grab it. Saylor played out slack as Tunks rolled the two survivors into the rescue basket. Tunks stayed behind in the sea, as there was not enough room in the basket for three. Saylor raised them to the cabin door where he and Mark Milne assisted them into the helicopter. The basket was lowered once again to recover Tunks from the violent seas. Again the winds made it difficult. Finally after multiple passes, Jeff grabbed the basket and rolled in.

"Swimmer Hurt"

Just then another of the williwaw blasts grabbed the helicopter and slammed it backwards. The basket was yanked from the crest of one wave with Tunks in it only to crash at thirty miles an hour into the face of the next wave and again into the next wave as Whiddon applied maximum power to stop the helicopter. Seeing Tunks smash in to the waves, Saylor thought that his friend had surely been killed. As it was, he received a badly bruised back that required hospitalization. Finally the pilot brought the helicopter under control and Tunks was hoisted safely aboard. The flight back to the air station was a quick one with the tailwinds. On post-flight it was discovered that the helicopter fuselage had stress ripples in the skin. The transmission, with multiple over-torques, had to be replaced.

Awards
Distinguished Flying Crosses
I was fortunate to be in the audience when Vice Admiral Costello and Nelson presented all five crewmembers the Distinguished

Flying Cross in a ceremony on the hanger deck of the Sitka Air Station. At the end of the formal ceremony Jim Blades came to the microphone with his son Clint. He picked his son up and held him to the mike where Clint said simply in his little boy voice, "Thank you for saving my life." There was not a dry eye in the house, including mine.

Alaska Award for Bravery-Heroism
The crew subsequently received many other awards including Tunks being selected for the Coast Guard Foundation Chester Bender Award for heroism. The crew also received the Alaska Award for Bravery-Heroism from Alaska Governor Steve Cowper. This was the first time a military crew had been so recognized since the award was created in 1965.[5]

Blue Bird rescue crew receives Alaska Bravery -Heroism Award from Governor Cowper (Courtesy Sitka Sentinel)

---

5   ibid, 102

Why Does the Coast Guard Do Search and Rescue (SAR)?

SAR History.

The earliest records of an organized group to rescue those in peril at sea, was on a volunteer basis paid for by non-governmental means. Its roots can be traced to the Massachusetts Humane Society founded in 1785 using as its model the Royal Humane Society of England. The Federal Government became involved with Federal funding with $5,000 in the 1847 Lighthouse Service budget for furnishing lighthouses with means for rendering assistance. Between 1848 and 1854, $92,500 was appropriated for establishing 137 lifeboats stations on the Atlantic Coast and Great lakes. Volunteers did the manning of these lifeboats, often housed in crude shacks along the shore. The system was plagued with vandalism and unreliability.[6]

Actual Federal ownership of the search and rescue mission can be traced to 1878 when the U.S. Lifesaving Service (USLS) was established in the Treasury Department under the able management of General Superintendent Sumner I. Kimball. Although in the same Federal department, the Revenue Marine was separate from the USLS.[7] The Revenue Marine, although not specifically charged with SAR, nevertheless provided assistance in keeping with the tradition that any seafaring ship in position to assist must respond to those in peril. In the 1830's Treasury Secretary McLane formally initiated a program of "winter cruises" by the Revenue Cutters to be on the lookout for vessels in distress. In 1915 the Revenue Cutter Service and the U. S. Lifesaving Service were officially merged to become the U. S. Coast Guard.[8]

Search and rescue is the mission with which the Coast Guard is most often associated. Both the national coverage of the rescue of 34,000 persons in danger during the hurricane Katrina recovery and Kevin Costner's movie The Guardian have

---

6   Kaplan and Hunt, 187-8

7   Commandant (G-IPA), *Coast Guard Organizational History Overview*, Washington D.C., 1

8   Kaplan and Hunt, 188

underscored this awareness. It's somewhat of a paradox that if many of the other missions accomplish their goals then SAR would be greatly reduced. Aids to Navigation, Boating Safety, Merchant Vessel Safety, Port Security, and vessel traffic systems especially are aimed at trying to prevent seafarers from standing into danger. Often human error, natural phenomenon or just bad luck intervenes, especially in the cold and lonely waters of Alaska resulting in persons in distress.

Search And Rescue In Alaska

My third assignment in Alaska was Chief of Search and Rescue (OSR) for the Seventeenth District from July 1982 to July 1984 after which I left to be the Commanding Officer of Coast Guard Air Station Borinquen, Puerto Rico. Talk about a change of scenery! My turn as OSR was challenging. It started the day I took over with the crash and destruction of a C-130 and the loss of two young lives. There were to be more fatalities during my two-year tour. The overall numbers for Coast Guard search and rescue in Alaska aren't that impressive as the annual number of cases runs just over 1,000. Coast Guard Air Station Miami alone exceeds these numbers annually. The severity of the conditions, however, often makes them some of the most challenging. Alaskan weather, water temperature and great distances all enter into the equation challenging Coast Guard responders on the last frontier.

Who's In Charge?

When someone gets into trouble in Alaska, it becomes the responsibility of the Coast Guard if it occurs over water. In Southeast Alaska, the Service is also responsible for overland search and rescue involving lost hunters, logging accidents, missing hikers, medical emergencies, and the list goes on. The U. S. Air Force has the responsibility for overland search and rescue in the remainder of the state except for the Aleutians where again the Coast Guard has the lead. The Alaska State troopers share over land rescue responsibility but have limited resources. One time in Kodiak I had to do a night flight into a village to medevac a drunk female who had caught her finger in a beer can and nearly severed it.

Rescue Assets

Coast Guard resources for search and rescue in Alaska (2011 figures) include:
- Coast Guard Air Station Kodiak (Six C-130's, four H-60's, and five HH-65's)
- CGAS Sitka (three H-60's)

CG 110 Patrol Boat

Patrol Boats
- USCG Cutter *Anacapa* (Petersburg)
- USCG Cutter *Liberty* (Juneau)
- USCG Cutter *Long Island* (Valdez)
- USCG Cutter *Mustang* (Seward)

- USCG Cutter *Naushon* (Ketchikan)
- USCG Cutter *Roanoke Island* (Homer)

Buoy Tenders:
- USCG Cutter *Anthony Petit* (Ketchikan)
- USCG Cutter *Elderberry* (Petersburg)
- USCG Cutter *Hickory* (Homer)
- USCG Cutter *Maple* (Sitka)
- USCG Cutter *Spar* (Kodiak)
- USCG Cutter *Sycamore* (Cordova)

Recently the first high endurance cutter was permanently assigned to Alaska with the USCG Cutter *Munroe,* a 378' cutter home ported in Kodiak. The new Medium Endurance Cutter USCGC *Alex Haley* is also assigned to Kodiak. In addition there are small boat stations in Juneau, Ketchikan, and Valdez. There are often two high endurance cutters assigned to Alaskan Patrol for fisheries enforcement. As was the case in the C-130 crash on Attu, these resources can be utilized for SAR if needed

Coast Guard Auxiliary
The civilian arm of the Coast Guard, the Auxiliary, aids the active duty arm immensely. The Auxiliary members are volunteers who use their own boats, aircraft, radios and other equipment to assist the active duty crews with their missions. One example is taking over tows once in protected waters. In Alaska there are 400 Auxiliary members in flotillas in Juneau, Ketchikan, Kodiak, Whittier, Seward and Anchorage.

Chapter Ten

Aids to Navigation

Aids to Navigation (ATON) is an important marine safety mission for the mariner. There is an entire fleet of black-hulled buoy tenders servicing, setting, checking, replacing batteries on buoys and shore aids, plus any number of other routine but critical responsibilities. Helicopters are often used to take ATON teams into remote sites to do maintenance on aids. Sometimes it can be dangerous as the following story demonstrates.

An Aids To Navigation Story - The Destruction of the Scotch Cap Light

Survivors of the event reported that suddenly the building started shaking and groaning like it was in pain. It was the middle of the night, 0130 on 1 April 1946, April Fools Day, but this was no joke. This was an earthquake that lasted for about a half a minute, but it probably seemed like an hour. The shaking made a mess of things like earthquakes do.

The location was the direction finder station and lighthouse at Scotch Cap located on the eastern side of Unimak Pass. This is where the Alaska Peninsula ends and the Aleutian Islands start. It's a seemingly forsaken place, but an important one, as this is where ships transit between the Bering Sea and the Gulf of Alaska. The direction finder station and the lighthouse keep ships off the rocks if they are good seamen. Scotch Cap was originally lit in June of 1903 and was the first coastal light built in Alaska.

The crew was frightened but knew they were in volcano country, which meant earthquakes. The log indicates that the direction finder station personnel talked to the five-person Scotch Cap Light crew below the direction finder station and only about 40 feet above the crashing waves. The light personnel reported that they had been shaken such that it seemed the floor would come up but had suffered no apparent damage.[1]

Scotch Cap Light after Tsunami

Slightly less than a half hour, at 0157, there was a second jolt. This one was shorter in duration but seemed more powerful.

1   Ed Moreth, PAC, *Tsunami*, (Juneau Alaska, Alaska Bear, 4 August 1990) 40-1

Again the two groups of Coast Guardsmen checked on each other. The lighthouse personnel said they were going to call the Navy Radio Station at Dutch Harbor to see if there was news about the earthquake.[2]

At 0218 the world ended for the lighthouse and its five-man crew. Survivors from the direction finder station reported that there was a terrible roaring sound followed immediately by a heavy blow on the side of the building, and the recreation room where they were all gathered was suddenly ankle deep in water. They attempted to contact the lighthouse crew, but there was no answer. At first light they discovered why. Scotch Cap Light House and its crew quarters were completely gone. The concrete structure had been ripped from its foundation as if by a giant hand.

For the next three weeks search parties scoured the rugged shoreline five miles in both directions from the light. One body was located and identified as Petty Officer First Class Paul Ness. Other body parts were located including a decapitated and disemboweled corpse that could not be identified. The remains of Ness were buried in a single grave and the parts of the others were buried in a common grave. The graves are located at a site 300 yards apart from the light they gave their lives for.[3]

---

2   ibid

3   Hoban Sanford, Chief Radio Electrician, USCG, *Memorandum*, (Coast Guard Stories, www.jacksjoint.com/scotch_cap_light)

Scotch Cap Light following tidal wave

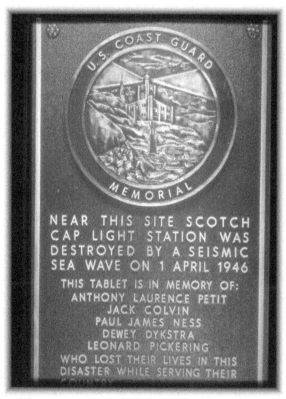

Memorial tablet to the crew lost at Scotch Cap Light

This memorial was displayed in the District Commander's office in the Federal building in Juneau.

The officer in Charge of the Light was Chief Boatswain's Mate Anthony Petit. The Coast Guard was later to name a buoy tender, the USCGC *Anthony Petit*, in his honor.

Why Is the Coast Guard Involved With Aids to Navigation?

History

ATON as a mission of the Coast Guard has the oldest roots of Federally funded public service.[4] Providing navigational assistance for mariners was originally a territorial or Colonial Governmental responsibility until the late 1790's when the Treasury Department was formed. Prior to that, the first lighthouse, Boston Light, was built on Little Brewster Island. The first Federally funded light to be built was in 1792 at Cape Henry Virginia.

The U. S. Lighthouse Service was established within Treasury on 7 August 1789 to take over operation of twelve colonial lighthouses. The Lighthouse Service became part of the Coast Guard on 1 July 1939 when President Roosevelt surprised both services in announcing the merger.[5]

Short Range ATON

The modern Coast Guard maintains approximately 97,000 short-range aids to navigation. It also operates eleven Vessel Traffic Systems including Vessel Traffic System Valdez.

The Short Range Aids to navigation include:

- Buoys
- Beacons
- Lights
- Lighthouses
- Ranges
- Sound signals (horns, bells, gongs, and whistles)
- Radar-reflecting devices

---

4   Kaplan and Hunt, 97

5   ibid

The scope is extensive when you realize it encompasses 95,000 miles of coastline and 25,000 miles of navigable rivers. In one of the more bizarre and little known responsibilities, the Coast Guard is responsible for approval of the location and plans for bridges and causeways constructed across navigable waters of the United States. This includes regulation of drawbridge operations to balance both land and marine transportation needs. The duty was taken over from the Army Corps of Engineers when the Service was moved into the Department of Transportation in 1967.[6]

Electronic Aids to Navigation
The Radio Aids to Navigation program has operated electronic aids around the world including Germany, Thailand, Turkey, Vietnam, Iceland and even the tiny Kure Atoll. The Radio Aids program actually encompasses three separate systems: 1) Differential Global Positioning System (DGPS), 2) LORAN – C, and 3) radio beacons.

Aids to Navigation in Alaska
The modern day ATON mission in Alaska is comprised of radio aids to navigation, short-range aids to navigation, vessel traffic systems and bridge administration. While this might seem to be somewhat of an uninteresting mission, in Alaska it's anything but. The operational assets of the Service that are responsible for maintaining this system are the buoy tenders, aids to navigation teams and the support structure, including industrial bases and the district Aids to Navigation Branch that manages the system. The most elemental navigational aids are the various colored buoys that are the street signs for the mariners. Alaska has nearly 34,000 miles of shoreline. Making sure that the buoys are on station and "watching properly" is a serious job.

Alaska ATON Numbers
In Alaska there are 180-lighted buoys and 234 unlighted buoys standing watch in its waters. There are also 631 lights and 239 day beacons maintained by the six buoy tenders assigned, and

---

6   USCG Fact File, Bridge Administration, (COMDT G-OPT)

the helicopter assisted aids to navigation teams known as Flying ANTS. Alaska has sixteen lighthouses. These are all automated now, but back in the days when there were crews assigned, normally four at each lighthouse, the logistics to sustain them was a major task. Some of my favorite missions out of Kodiak were to fly movies and perishable supplies to Hinchinbrook and Cape St. Elias Lights.

Long Range Aids To Navigation

Another component of the aids to navigation mission in Alaska are the radio navigation continuous all-weather electronic Long Range Navigation or LORAN stations. LORAN was a product of WWII when it was considered somewhat of a black box miracle. LORAN consists of high power electronic signals emitted from 600-foot towers. The LORAN-A of WWII was replaced in 1980 by LORAN-C with accuracy for maritime users of one-quarter mile. With the onset of the Global Position System, LORAN is being phased out. At this writing there are no manned LORAN stations in Alaska, and they have all been placed in caretaker status.

During my time on active duty there were six LORAN stations in Alaska. These stations needed to be located where they were free from interference and their locations reflect this isolation. The stations were on Attu Island, St Paul Island, Pt. Clarence south of Nome, Tok Junction, Narrow Cape forty miles from Kodiak, and South of Yakutat. All of these stations were manned by military members of the Coast Guard for a year's tour of duty. Their supply and support fell on various managers in the Coast Guard to carry out. The Aids to Navigation mission area is critical to the safety of the mariner and our merchant fleet, on which our nation depends.

Chapter Eleven

Ice Operations

Operating U.S. icebreakers is becoming a lost art. For one thing they are very expensive ships to build and operate. Consequently, in tight budget years they are at risk of not being funded. In 2012 the U.S. had one operational polar icebreaker, the *Healey*. But as our capabilities decrease, the current needs are increasing. Alaska's Lt. Gov. Mead Treadwell testified before the House Transportation Committee on 1 December 2011 that he felt that Alaska was naked should there be a problem with the increased shipping in the Bering Strait. According to the 2010 Naval Operations Concept, the Coast Guard would need ten icebreakers to maintain the "continuous presence" called for in that study.[1] As long as there is ice in the Arctic we will need icebreakers.

An Ice Operations Story; Breaking the Ice ARCTIC WEST - 67
Background
Ice brought me to Alaska the first time. The mission was a rather minor one in terms of resources and public awareness. This was the Ice Operations mission also known as Polar Operations. A few specialized vessels called icebreakers carry out Polar Operations.

---

1   Philip Ewing *Alaska appeals for icebreakers*, (Naval, save and invest. org 2011)

These are not elegant ladies but rather beefy, long-legged ships designed to operate in ice and the polar regions.

U. S. Priority

Unlike the Russians, icebreakers have never been a high priority to the U.S. government. In fact, as I write this the National Science Foundation is managing the polar icebreakers, and one is in inactive status, chained to the dock so to speak, for lack of funding. This wasn't always the case. Back in WWII, icebreakers were important for defense operations in Greenland and northern waters. Originally the U.S. Navy operated most icebreakers, but in 1967 the responsibility was transferred to the Coast Guard. At the time the icebreaking fleet consisted of five resources. They were the *Glacier* and the *Burton Island*, and the three Wind Class breakers, *Northwind, Westwind,* and *Eastwind.* These five are now all razorblades, which means they've been permanently retired. They've been replaced with three more powerful Polar Class icebreakers, the *Polar Sea*, the *Polar Star* and the newest and most sophisticated ice-cruncher, the *Healy.*

Helicopter pilots come to icebreaking by the back door, basically the hangar door. My own experience began in 1967 at the CG Air Station in Astoria, Oregon where I was assigned after earning my Navy wings in Pensacola, Florida in December 1965 as Coast Guard helicopter pilot #563. In the spring of 1966, CGAS Astoria's inventory of three HH-52A, Sea Guard Sikorsky helicopters, was joined by two bubble-bell helicopters designated the HH-13N. These two little helicopters had as their primary mission to provide helicopter support for the icebreaker USCGC *Northwind* (WAGB-282), home ported in Seattle. Those of us at Astoria realized that we had suddenly picked up a new additional job, that of polar operations (Polar Ops) pilots.

We subsequently began providing flight crews to the USCGC *Northwind* for Arctic deployments in 1966. Too junior and inexperienced to make the first trip, I was glad not to go. Not knowing much about icebreakers, I did know that they went out for very long deployments to places that were very cold. It sounded like a losing proposition to me. Little did I know how much fun it would be when subsequently selected to make the second deployment in the summer of 1967.

Arctic West - 67
Players
The *Northwind's* Arctic West-67 air detachment consisted of three pilots and five enlisted rates to fly and maintain the two helicopters when they were deployed. I was the junior pilot. The other two were LCDR Dick Burns, the senior aviator, and LT Ron Addison.

Arctic West Helicopter
The equipment we would be flying were two bubble bell helicopters. The senior aviator for the deployment decided to name them Snoopy and the Red Baron. I thought that was unprofessional but kept my mouth shut. The little bird had an enclosed boom and was powered by a Lycoming gasoline engine controlled by a throttle on the end of the collective control. Its instrumentation was somewhat limited, but it did have a gyro stabilized artificial horizon gauge. This was to prove invaluable when months later I encountered a phenomenon known as a "white out" where the sky, surface and horizon all blend together. The fact that this situation could cause vertigo is an understatement. The bird was visual flight rules only and not authorized for instrument conditions. Instrument conditions are what you have when flying in clouds or low visibility such as heavy snow and you have no visible horizon to tell you your aircraft attitude. Having no stabilization equipment, it was a hands-on aircraft whenever its rotors were turning.

There was also no heater, as it had been removed long before because of weight constraints. We kept warm when flying in the Arctic by wearing neoprene wet suits. This worked for everything except my hands, which even though wearing cold weather flight gloves, were always freezing during flight. Also not being able to release the flight controls for any length of time meant that you couldn't even rub your hands together for warmth.

HH-13N and ground crew getting ready at Sand Point Naval Air Station

The helicopter was capable of water landings with its rubber pontoons attached to rigid skids. Because of the skids, it could be moved around on the ground only by attaching small ground handling wheels after each flight. We practiced training on the helicopters preparing for the deployment. It was a fun aircraft to fly, and I had flown about 30 hours in a similar model, the H-13M, in Naval flight training. That was the primary helicopter training aircraft at the time.

Deployment

Finally the time came for our deployment. We actually left a week early because the senior aviator thought we needed to work as a team for a week in Seattle. We flew Snoopy and the Red Baron from Astoria to the old Naval Air Station at Sand Point early in June 1967, while the enlisted crew drove up with all our spare parts and personal equipment. After working out of Sand Point for a week, we boarded the *Northwind* and departed on 15 June for four months in the Arctic. The actual flight to the *Northwind* was not a good start for me.

The weather was rainy with low ceilings, typical of Seattle. Remembering the limited instrumentation, I was flying single pilot with a crewman in the right seat, the other two pilots had gone ahead in the Red Baron. Attempting to follow in Snoopy I quickly lost them in the poor visibility caused by patchy clouds, fog and drizzle. The plan had been to fly the western shore of Lake Washington to the ship canal and follow it through Lake Union to Puget Sound, then southbound to the pier where the *Northwind* awaited. Knowing there was high terrain and power lines across the ship canal to the west of Lake Union caused me some concern. Worried that we would need to go low to stay visual, and not wanting to end the deployment before it even started by flying into high tension wires, I elected to land in Lake Union and wait for conditions to improve. My crew and I spent about 30 minutes water taxiing, keeping an eye out for any curious boaters, until the weather lifted and we could continue the flight. It turned out fairly easy to locate the *Northwind*. It was basically a giant white bathtub with a helicopter deck. Once I found it I came aboard for our great adventure.

The Icebreaker Northwind

I fell in love with the breaker from the very beginning. It was a fat, dumpy girl for sure, but a beauty to behold in the ice. She was 269 feet long and 64 feet wide, which made her very beamy (wide) for a basically short ship. All the weight she carried made her have a loaded draft of nearly thirty feet.

The *Wind* could carry a lot of stuff. For one thing she had a large crew of twenty officers and 195 enlisted ship's company. We of course added even more people and stuff. The *Northwind* class could carry 700,000 gallons of fuel providing a range of 24,000 miles. Because we were going to make several port calls in Juneau and Kodiak before we actually started our Arctic West missions, the *Wind* was loaded down with a thousand cases of beer, fifteen cases of cigarettes, and 1,147 cases of soda. This was stuff that was expensive to ship to Alaska commercially and was destined for the Coast Guard stores, called exchanges, in Juneau and Kodiak where we were scheduled to make port calls.

The *Northwind* was no fast lady, as her maximum speed in 1967 was 13.4 knots, and that was probably going down hill. Her 6500 tons was pushed through the water by a diesel electric power plant consisting of six Fairbanks Morse ten-cylinder diesels driving six Westinghouse generators, which in turn drove three electric motors yielding a shaft horsepower of 12,000 SHP. The *Northwind* class originally had three propellers, two aft and one forward. The forward prop was intended not so much for propulsion but to suck water from under the ice, enabling the breaker to more efficiently break her way.

How It Works
The mechanics of an icebreaker were fascinating. Admittedly her shape was not a destroyer, sleek like a greyhound. The purpose of this design was to avoid vertical sides to prevent the ice from crushing the ship were it to become stuck, which happened often. As the ice pressure would build, the *Northwind* sloping sides would result in the ship being squeezed up like toothpaste from a tube. She also had a heeling system, which could move a lot of liquid from one side to the other, rocking the boat again to prevent freezing in. All of this worked great in the ice but meant that the ship was a terrible sea keeper in any kind of a swell. She wallowed like a pig. This could be dangerous and on at least one occasion that I know of, a person on watch on the bridge was violently thrown across the wheelhouse and was killed.

At the business end of the ship was a very gradual sloping bow. The icebreaker did not break ice so much by splitting it as she did by sliding up on it and using her great weight to crush down through. In ice over a couple of feet thick, the *Northwind* would gradually lose her momentum and have to back down to get a run at it again. With all systems in operation, the ship would be porposing up and down, rolling, backing and ramming her way through the ice. It was impressive.

Snoopy and the Red Baron in their cozy hanger
with the telescoping hanger retracted

Aviation Detachment Purpose
Our role as the aviation detachment was to be the eyes of the
ship when in the ice. We also did logistics work such as picking
up mail and transporting personnel in an emergency. Whenever
the ship was in the ice, we tried to have a helicopter airborne
checking out leads in the ice. A lead is a channel of open water
between large pieces of ice floes. Sometimes these leads would go
on for miles. Other times they would end in a thick pressure ridge
where wind had piled the ice up. The *Northwind* could not break
through these pressure ridges when they got too thick. We as the
ship's eyes would fly the leads and check them out to avoid going
down a blind alley so to speak. One of my contributions to all this
was the suggestion to mix green dye marker crystals with water
and carry them beneath our aircraft seats in glass oceanographic
sample bottles. When we came to a decision point for the ship to
go one way or the other, we would throw out a bottle to break on
the ice. It would leave a large green florescent mark if the bottle
broke, which they usually did. We would then radio the breaker
of the position and what to do when they got there.

The *Northwind* had a unique hanger, known as the birdhouse, which retracted on tracks to expose the flight deck. When flight operations were over and during normal transit operations, Snoopy and the Red Baron would be chained side-by-side, nose to tail, snug in their little hanger. The hanger in actual practice took some getting used to. Each side moved independently with two electric motors. It was very easy to get out of synch and jam the mechanism.

Flight Operations

Underway

Arctic West officially started with the *Northwind*'s departure from Seattle on 15 June 1967. The first four days included loading explosives at the Naval Weapons Station at Indian Island across from Port Townsend, Washington. We then sailed the Inside Passage heading for Juneau. En route we had several days of flight operations getting the ship's company used to operating their little birds.

Alaska Port Call – Juneau

We arrived in Juneau on the afternoon of 19 June. We sailed up Gastineau Channel into Juneau on a beautiful sunny day. The three thousand plus high terrain of the mainland to the north, and the mountains of Douglas Island to the south form the channel. Both sides had dozens of waterfalls cascading down the mountains to the sea. It was truly spectacular. We moored at the dock at the Government Pier right in down town Juneau, across from what is now Centennial Hall. The view was mixed to put it politely.

On a hill, above the docks, was the three story, 14,400 square foot Governor's mansion, built in 1912 for $40,000. In 1967 it was going through a renovation to add two guest suites and a bedroom to the third floor that had been intended for a territorial museum, but was never built. Between the mansion and the waterfront were shanties and WWII type corrugated steel Quonset huts. This was unfortunately typical of the impression Alaska left on visitors. Its gorgeous natural beauty was too often marred by man-made squalor and trash. As we flew along the Alaskan coast later on in the deployment, we saw so many rusting 55-gallon drums left abandoned that we began calling them the Alaska state flower.

After two days playing tourist and offloading most of our soft drinks and beer we departed Juneau on 21 June heading for Kodiak Island. One of my most vivid memories of the Juneau visit was coming out of a bar nearly at midnight into twilight that was light enough to read by.

Port Call - Kodiak

We arrived at Kodiak on the morning of 23 June faced with dense fog and low water. The piers at Kodiak were in a small body of water known as Old Woman's Bay. To get there required doing a 180-degree turn around Nyman's Peninsula, which was no small feat in the fog. The tidal range in Kodiak is approximately 10 feet, and rocky pinnacles and mud flats await the unwary. The *Northwind* skipper, the prudent seaman he was, put over a ship's small boat with a portable Fathometer to lead the ship slowly into Old Woman's Bay where we were to moor. I subsequently learned that this was a technique used in the olden sailing days in the Arctic when charts were notoriously inaccurate, using a hand held lead line in a ship's boat in lieu of the fathometer.

The primary installation on Kodiak in 1967 was the US Naval Station Kodiak. The Coast Guard Air Station was a tenant as were two Coast Guard Cutters and a buoy tender. It was also the headquarters of the USN Commander, Alaskan Sea Frontier. Alaska had been a gigantic headache for the Navy in WWII with its great distances, dangerous weather, lousy charts and difficult logistics. The Navy made the decision to leave Kodiak and all of mainland Alaska in 1972 and transferred administrative responsibility to the Navy headquarters in Seattle. This left the Coast Guard with a large landlord responsibility for a major installation.

We had an enjoyable two days of liberty in Kodiak where two of my Academy classmates were stationed with their wives. Rightly nicknamed the Emerald Isle, Kodiak is a fascinating place. At 100 miles long, it is second only to the big island of Hawaii as the largest island in the United States. Although it is fifty miles wide, there is no place on the island that is more than fifteen miles from salt water due to the thousand of inlets and bays contained in the Kodiak Archipelago. It is also very mountainous with steep cliffs arising from the thousands of inlets. It is an outdoorsman's paradise with bountiful hunting and fishing. It is also home to the some of the largest brown bears in the world so caution when afield is always wise. Kodiak is also infamous for its unpredictable and changeable weather, which also can be life threatening for the unprepared. All of this I was to learn first hand.

There were five phases for Arctic West 67. Phase five was classified, and as a junior officer I had no need to know, so I still don't know specifically what it was. It recalls the old CIA joke, "If I told you what I did, I'd have to kill you." I can guess however that it had something to do with the Soviets, as the Cold War was still very active.

Phase One - Stuff for the DEW line

This Phase was officially known as the Mackenzie River Sealift. It entailed providing icebreaker support for commercial vessels engaged in the re-supply of several of the Distance Early Warning (DEW) stations.

Snoopy visits a typical Distance Early Warning (DEW) station

In 1967, a series of fifty-eight very remote radar sites stretched across the top of Alaska and Canada. This was the Distant Early Warning system or DEW line, which belonged to DOD but were contractor operated and manned. President Eisenhower ordered the system's construction in 1954. The sites were constructed under extremely difficult circumstances from 1955 to 1957 because the season for water travel was limited due to year round ice, not to mention the high winds and freezing temperatures.

How the Resupply Worked
Approximately forty people manned each DEW line site that we visited by helicopter during AW-67. These crews were primarily civilians, however there was often a Canadian Officer as liaison. One of the other pilots traded his orange winter flight suit for a much better purple two-piece Canadian flight suit. I was really jealous. It was a logistical nightmare to keep these remote places supplied, especially with fuel for their generators. The logistics were accomplished by sealift on a contract basis.

Normally in the summer, the ice recedes from the shore enough for a non-ice strengthened vessel to transit without problems. Like everything in the Arctic, there are exceptions. Ice is very fickle and literally blows with the wind. If there is a prolonged onshore blow, the ice can move in and trap an unsuspecting ship. That's why the *Northwind* was on call during this period, and it generated a lot of interesting ice breaking. The first divert for this phase occurred while the ship was off Point Barrow loading supplies. On the evening of 9 August, the *Northwind* received a call that the USNS *Pinnebog*, a Canadian operated transfer tanker ship engaged in the Mackenzie River Sealift, was beset in the ice and needed assistance. The *Northwind* immediately began offloading all the excess cargo and made preparations for heading east to assist.

Thick sea ice was encountered, but the *Northwind* made slow and steady progress, arriving eventually at the location of the *Pinnebog* on 19 August. The *Northwind* was able to circle the *Pinnebog* and break the cargo ship free. We then escorted the ship for the next two weeks as she did her re-supply.

Frank Broderick and barge stuck in ice

SAR in the Ice

On 1 September the small Arctic freighter *Frank Broderick* which was towing a small barge, requested the *Northwind*'s assistance. It also was beset by ice. The *Northwind* relieved the *Broderick* of her tow, taking it close aboard her own stern, and the *Northwind* led them both to open water. Towing the barge in the ice presented some difficulty. If the towline were too long, ice would come between the *Northwind* and the barge. The scope of the tow then had to be fairly short. At one point, when some heavy ice stopped the breaker, the barge continued under its own momentum and struck the stern of the *Northwind*. The breaker with her heavy hull suffered little more than a dent, the barge suffered extensive damage to her port corner and a cargo gate. By 7 September, the assistance of the *Northwind* was no longer required and we departed to return to Point Barrow to once again load supplies.

Phase Two - The Rock

There is an unusual granite formation sitting in the middle of the Bering Straits approximately twenty miles west of Cape Prince of Wales. This great piece of rock, known as Fairway Rock, rises 534 feet above sea level and is uninhabited by man. However. It is home to an estimated 35,000 seabirds, and they all hate helicopters. The *Northwind* on an earlier deployment in 1964 established an unmanned oceanographic station in the fifty-meter deep waters adjacent to the rock. A radioisotope thermoelectric generator located on the top of the rock provided power for the station. Our mission was to fly technicians to the top of Fairway Rock to replace the strontium 90 batteries.

Fairway Rock in the Bering Straits

We arrived at the site in the late afternoon of 1 July with good flying conditions. The Captain elected to wait until the next day to tackle the project. Bad decision. Rule number one: never pass up good weather in the Arctic. The weather moved in that night and the next morning the top of Fairway was in fog and stayed so until a week later on 7 July. When we finally got adequate weather to fly to the top of the rock we discovered another sobering challenge, the birds. They would actually dive at us on approach. I was sure that some actually flew through my rotor path. Fortunately we recorded no bird strikes. Once we began this phase, things went fast. We conducted operations for twenty hours straight, completing seventeen sorties. In all we flew forty-two hours and logged 134 passenger miles for the project.

One of the most striking atmospheric phenomena I encountered was sitting on top of the rock with the wind blowing sea fog up the near vertical sides. I was literally looking at a moving wall of fog rising vertically directly in front of the helicopter. It was one of many spectacular natural phenomena I enjoyed on the trip. We finally got the generators recharged, had some other maintenance performed, and flew our own birds into their nest on the *Northwind*.

Phase Three - Science

The third phase was scientific. There was much we didn't know about the Polar Regions, and one of the key arguments for justifying the icebreakers was to provide a platform for scientific research there. It's still true to this day over forty years later, and it is even more important in this period of global warming and drastic changes in the Arctic. This mission started on 8 July when we flew into Port Clarence LORAN Station south of Nome on Norton Sound. Remembering that map of Alaska superimposed on the lower 48, Port Clarence would be in South Dakota.

Port Clarence was one of six Long Range Aids to Navigation (LORAN) stations in Alaska. Each was in a remote location with the most striking feature being the 600-foot tall tower at each station. I can remember vividly the footprint of guy wires leading out from the towers and thinking how they could play havoc for the unwary pilot. Each station also had a small airstrip for logistics flights, and we picked up a field party of four scientists from the University of Washington and three Coast Guard Oceanographic personnel, making several trips with both helicopters. Their project would take approximately three weeks, and it was a crushing bore for the fliers as there were no flight operations involved other than transporting the personnel to and from the *Northwind*.

The Scientific Studies Accomplished

The scientific studies entailed four different areas of investigation. The first was studying the circulation and interaction of waters between the northern Bering and Chukchi Seas. They were also measuring the Bering Sea flow, the exchange of water, salt and heat between the two seas, and finally the tidal wave patterns. To accomplish the investigations, the *Northwind* had to anchor at eighty-three stations. The depth rarely exceeded fifty meters, approximately 157 feet. The stations were both north and south of the Bering Straits, where the distance between Russia and the United States is only about three miles. At each station the scientists took samples of the water from the bottom to the surface at five-meter intervals. They recorded the temperature, salinity and oxygen level for each station. This portion of the deployment was considered a great success and generated much scientific data.

SAR – *Vessel Trapped by Ice*

This phase was interrupted on 23 July when the *Northwind* received word that a small Canadian research ship, the CSS *Richardson*, had been caught in the ice when the wind shifted. She reported herself in danger of being crushed and requested assistance. The position of the distress was five miles northwest of Pt. Barrow. Plotting it out, this was approximately 300 miles away, much of it through ice. The CSS *Richardson* we found out was a ninety-foot steel hulled research vessel with a beam of twelve feet. There were seven persons onboard, and they reported that the pressure of the ice was forcing the ship out of the water, and they were listing 40 degrees,

The *Northwind* immediately pulled up anchor and headed north. About mid-afternoon the next day, we were within flying distance of the *Richardson,* and we launched both helicopters with me flying one. The *Northwind* was in 100% (known as 10/10) coverage of solid brown ice. One of the things I learned was that the old weathered ice was often mud colored. I could only conjure whether this was from wind blown dust or if the ice had sometimes been grounded, I don't know.

The Canadian research ship *Richardson* trapped in the ice with
the Canadian icebreaker *Camsell* in the background

After a short flight we located the *Richardson* and gave the course
to the *Northwind*. Nearby we discovered a bright red Canadian
Coast Guard ship, the *Camsell*, which had proceeded from the east
to attempt to assist. The pressure ice was too thick for the *Camsell*
and she stood by as the *Northwind* proceeded to break out the
Richardson. Once this was accomplished all three vessels hove to
for the evening to wait for lessening of the ice pressure.

The morning of 25 July the ice had eased some, and the
Northwind led the *Richardson* to the *Camsell*, which took the
small boat in tow. Later on that day the *Camsell* again had trouble
with the ice so the *Northwind* pulled her into a special feature, the
stern notch. This is an effective way to tow a vessel in ice by pulling
the bow of the vessel to be towed into the notch on the stern of
the breaker. This being done, the *Northwind* towed the *Camsell*,
who in turn was towing the *Richardson*, to the edge of the ice pack
where the two vessels proceeded independently.

The *Northwind* then returned to the last oceanographic station
to complete Phase III.

Phase Four - T-3 - Fletcher's ice island
The figurehead mission of Arctic West-67 was to re-supply the manned Fletcher's Ice Island, referred to as T-3.

Background
The island was approximately seven miles by three miles, estimated to be 125 feet thick, and was named for USAF Col. Tom Fletcher who had first landed on T-3 in 1952. It drifted aimlessly throughout the Arctic Ocean. A manned research and weather station was eventually established there and manned from 1952 until 1978.

Arctic diesel in 55-gallon drums loaded and offloaded many times

The majority of the logistics to support the Island were normally flown in by the Air Force from Point Barrow Alaska or Thule Air Base, Greenland.

Northwind Attempts T-3 Resupply

This year the *Northwind* was to attempt the first surface re-supply, and we were to carry 45,855 lbs. of supplies for the power generators and other equipment. The load included thirty fuel bladders and tanks, twenty-four 55-gallon drums of lube oil and antifreeze, twenty-two fifty-foot sections of four-inch diameter rubber hose with various pumps and related equipment and 120,000 gallons of arctic diesel fuel. The Arctic had other ideas. Twice the *Northwind* was diverted for rescue missions and all this equipment had to be offloaded by ship's small boats and transferred to shore. Offshore Point Barrow it was too shallow for the *Northwind* to get within several miles of the shoreline.

Starting Late

The *Northwind* arrived off of Point Barrow on 10 September ready to resume the T-3 re-supply phase. The deck force once again re-loaded all the bladders, the 120,000 gallons of Arctic diesel fuel and the barrels of lubricant. This was no small task with the limitations of the equipment on hand. Finally the *Northwind* departed north 11 September. We had been delayed an entire month for the start of this mission due to other duties, and the temperature had dropped with the resulting increase in ice formation. The ice island was at eighty degrees north latitude when we left Barrow.

Looking Good

Initially things looked very good, and the helicopters were used extensively during this period. We were able to find open leads that allowed the ship to make good time. On 13 September we were in 10/10 ice coverage with a heavy concentration of Arctic pack ice that was from three to five feet thick and had an average of three inches of snow covering. Nevertheless, the *Northwind* continued making good time until 14 September. when things started to become more challenging. That morning we were at position 78-32-.5N and 161-31.9W in 9/10 coverage of polar ice. The conning officer attempted to pass through two large floes and got stuck with the pressure between them. This was the first time that the ship had actually been stuck, unable to heel or back down. The decision was made to attempt to use dynamite to loosen the pressure. Several attempts were unsuccessful although it put on a great show. Finally in the afternoon, after eight hours of being stuck, the ship broke free utilizing full astern engines and the heeling and trim systems, along with the use of dynamite.

Looking Not So Good

Up to this point, we had all been confident that we were going to be able to make T-3. Now we weren't so optimistic. Just to make sure that we understood how tentative operations in the Arctic could be. Mother Nature changed the weather on us. On the 14 September the wind changed from northerly to easterly, the temperatures dropped to below freezing and periods of heavy snow showers began. The ship's progress slowed considerably, and the helicopters were used continually for close-in conning, as it was difficult for the officer-of-the-deck to ascertain the optimum route without airborne recommendations.

On the 16 September, *Northwind* crossed the 79th parallel. We were in 10/10 coverage with medium, big and vast floes of Arctic pack varying from eight to fifteen feet in thickness. Progress now was measured in yards rather than in miles. We were making on average about five miles a day by constant backing and ramming. This began to take its toll. On the morning of the 16th, a crack, one-quarter inch wide and three and a half feet long was discovered in the bow shaft alley. Flooding was slight and emergency repairs were made. The icebreaking capabilities were only minimally impacted, and the attempt to reach Fletcher continued.

However, conditions worsened daily as the Arctic winter approached. The decision was made to heave to at night rather than to attempt proceeding without the helicopters being airborne.

Finally on 20 September the order was received to discontinue the attempt due to deteriorating weather, decreasing daylight and worsening ice conditions. At the time the *Northwind* was at 79-26.5N and 167-57W. Frustratingly, we were within thirty-five miles of T-3 but only progressing a few miles a day. This position was the furthest north that any western icebreaker had reached, although it was a milestone without substance. Reluctantly we turned south in an attempt to escape. The ice was thickening each day as the temperatures dropped. Morale was dropping having to abandon the mission after the tremendous effort on the part of the crew.

Looking Bad
On 23 September, day 101 of the deployment, the low morale turned to serious concern. A loud bang was heard throughout the ship. My shipboard roommate, Ensign Ned Lofton, was conning the ship. While backing down after losing forward momentum, he had the bad luck of getting a large piece of ice trapped between the stern and the starboard propeller. One of the three blades, weighing over a ton, broke off. This put us in the unenviable position of facing worsening conditions with reduced capability to handle them. We attempted to use the out-of-balance propeller but the vibration was horrendous. A person couldn't pour more than a half-cup of coffee without it sloshing out. At one time, the stub mast at the top of the main mast broke off and came crashing to the deck. Fortunately, no one was injured.

SAR – Icebreaker Needs Assistance
The decision was made to declare an emergency. Good luck! Here we were surrounded by 10/10 coverage of ice, getting thicker daily, and fifty percent power with no way to fix it. The only way to help an icebreaker in trouble is to summon another icebreaker. The Canadians immediately ordered their icebreaker *John A. McDonald* to attempt to assist us. Likewise, the USCGC *Staten Island* was directed to proceed and assist. The USCGC *Glacier*, in her homeport of Long Beach making preparations to deploy to Antarctica, was directed to prepare to assist as well. Unknown

to us, we became a hot news item. Not only were we in the ice, we were also in the dark. Remembering back to 1967, there were no communications satellites, no personal computers and no cell phones. The only news we got came over an ancient Teletype and was circulated for all to read. The news we got must have been somewhat filtered. I didn't know of the deadly Detroit riots resulting from the protests at the Democratic Convention until we got home. Also the phenomenon of the hit song by Bobbie Gentry, "Ode to Billie Joe," and the Tallahatchie Bridge was news to us.

We continued to slug it out trying to escape the ice but progress was agonizingly slow. We knew that help was on the way in the form of two US and one Canadian icebreaker, but feared that conditions would become too extreme due to the thickening ice. On Friday, 29 September, a meeting was held in the wardroom for all officers, and the possibility of wintering over was discussed. In this case all the ship's systems would be secured for long-term storage. When the snow had built up sufficiently to level off the ice, aircraft with skis would fly in and airlift the crew out. This could take a matter of months before conditions permitted. We didn't like the prospect, but we had plenty of fuel and whatever additional food we might need could be parachuted to us.

Our daily flights continued with the helicopters looking for the optimum route for the breaker to proceed but the options were limited. We were receiving help however. USN P-3 Orion long-range aircraft completing ice recon flights had occasionally broken the total silence of the Arctic sky. They were a welcome sight, as it got lonesome up there. Every now and then they would make an airdrop of a package containing newspapers and magazines. All hands devoured these ties with the outside. The flights became more frequent with the awareness of our difficulties. They proved to be a godsend. The perspective of the eyes in the skies allowed them to pass along some leads to the icebreakers coming to our rescue.

Help Arrives

With the assistance of the Navy recommendations and some favorable winds, we made rendezvous with the *John A. McDonald* and *Staten Island* on the morning of 3 October. What a grand sight to see the great orange Canadian breaker coming into view. We weren't home free yet, however. We still had over 180 miles to cover before we would be out of the Arctic pack. For the next five days we had constant helicopter conning alternating with our two birds and one on the *McDonald*. It was interesting to compare setting "flight quarters" between the two ships.

USCGC *Staten Island* and Canadian icebreaker
McDonald leading us home

The Canadian pilot would have one crewman help him push the helicopter out of their hanger and then proceed to strap his German Shepard dog into the co-pilot seat, get into his own seat and start the bird. We on the other hand, had a crash crew standing by with a charged fire hose, a boat crew at their stations, and various phone talkers and signals officers in attendance. In all we would have about fifty people in various duties. Our system was labor intensive but I would prefer it if a problem developed, like an aircraft fire.

"Watch It Mate, It's Sticky Out Here"

My most harrowing experience occurred on this phase of our adventure. I was turning up on the *Northwind* flight deck about to relieve the Canadian pilot of conning duties. He called me on the radio and said something like "Watch it Mate it's sticky out here." I no sooner took off than I found out what he meant. There was a low-lying ice fog that was not unusual. This time it was super cold moisture that froze the moment it touched something. That something was my orange helicopter. I noticed my windshield icing up almost instantly. More importantly the speed of the helicopter blades began slowing dramatically even though I had the full throttle on. An immediate controlled but hard landing on the ice resulted. A radio call to the *Northwind* explained the sudden landing along with the request that they get as close to me as possible. The ship crunched her way to me sitting on the ice. When it was close, I revved the maximum turns I could from the rotor system. I radioed the ship my plans to literally hop aboard and to dispense with the landing signals officer guiding me in.

Lifting the little bird into a quick hover, I slid over the flight deck and plopped it down. Immediately on landing, large pieces of ice came flying off the rotors and banged into the hanger and ship's superstructure. Fortunately no one was hit with the ice. The helicopter was wheeled into the heated hanger where it took several hours for the ice to melt off the fuselage, rotor hub and blades. Had this occurred at a higher altitude, I very likely would have crashed. I learned never to fly into ice clouds and much preferred the warmer places to fly like Florida and Puerto Rico.

Open Water

Finally on 8 October our little convoy joined up with the *Glacier* and later that afternoon hit open water. We then proceeded to Point Barrow where, for the third time, we off-loaded the Arctic diesel. For all I know that stuff may be still wandering around the Arctic. We then departed for the lower forty-eight.

The two helicopters departed the *Northwind* in the Straits of Juan de Fuca on 23 October and flew down the interstates and major highways to Astoria. The rest of the crew, with our personal gear, rode the ship into Pier 91 at Seattle and then headed for home by truck. We had been gone from home for 140 days. During that time we flew a total of 290 hours and 319 sorties. It was a fascinating experience.[2]

Why Does the Coast Guard Do Ice Operations?

An executive order issued in 1936 dictated national policy for using vessels in channels and harbors for icebreaking to facilitate commerce. In 1965 the national policy was outlined to consolidate all icebreakers in the Coast Guard. Prior to this time, the US Navy had operated icebreakers as well.[3] In polar regions icebreakers escort ships, provide logistics support to isolated installations and provide a platform for research. Domestically, the goal is to keep shipping lanes and ports open year round. Also the *Mackinaw* was operated exclusively on the Great Lakes to assist commerce in the winter months.

Ice Operations in Alaska.

There are no icebreakers home ported in Alaska, The newest icebreaker, the *USCGC Healy*, was commissioned in 2000 and is primarily intended for work in the Arctic but is home-ported in Seattle. At 420 feet length, overall, she is over 150 feet longer than the *Northwind* was. The *Healy* displaces 16,000 tons compared to the *Northwind*'s 6,515 tons. Interestingly they both have nearly identical drafts at just over twenty-nine feet.

---

2   USCGC Northwind (WAGB-282), 1967 Arctic Cruise Report

3   USCG Fact File, Ice Operations – Polar (PTO) and Domestic (DIO)

USCGC *Healy*

The *Healy* is basically a floating laboratory with over 5,000 sq. ft. of dedicated lab space, and can accommodate up to fifty scientists. The crew is nineteen officers and sixty-six enlisted and chief petty officers. The *Northwind,* on the other hand, had fourteen officers and 205 enlisted.

The Coast Guard in Alaska does not do icebreaking for commerce, although its six buoy tenders have limited icebreaking capability. Fortunately, most commercially viable ports in Alaska are ice free now in the winter, with the exception of Anchorage.

Chapter Twelve

Maritime Safety

It was December 2007, and I was sitting in the District Commander's office on the seventh deck (floor) of the Federal Building in Juneau. It was typical Juneau winter weather outside, windy, wet and wild. My visit was a courtesy call on the District Commander, Rear Admiral Brookes. The Admiral had greeted me in his BDU's (Battle Dress Uniform), which was a change from days past. It struck me that it was a good uniform to work in and certainly more military than the tie and cardigan that I use to wear on active duty when I worked down the hall fourteen years earlier.

I'd been in this office many times before. Sometimes it was routine, to brief the boss on an ongoing operation. Sometimes not so pleasant, as when one boss, Rear Admiral Knapp, was chewing me out. I always liked working for Dick Knapp. He was class of 1951 from the Academy and had a lot of operational time, including icebreaker command. The reason for the chewing was for a statement I made to a Seattle Post Intelligence reporter during the heat of an extended search for two missing fishing boats out of Dutch Harbor. The reporter asked me in a phone interview if I would prefer to have an air station out in the Aleutians. (That way we wouldn't have to make the long haul from Kodiak, over 300 miles, every time we got a distress call in the crab fleet.) I answered that it would be helpful. This of course made the front page of the Seattle PI. When that was read in Washington D.C.,

Knapp's Boss, the Chief of Operations, called and chewed him out about some Commander not making policy for the CG. The Alaskan congressional contingent had been putting pressure on the Coast Guard to build an air station in the Aleutians. Of course I, in turn, got a lesson in not sharing my opinions with someone who buys his ink by the barrel.

On this more pleasant courtesy call, I asked Brookes about his concerns as the person responsible for Coast Guard operations in Alaska. After a moment, he said his worst nightmare was a fire on board a super cruise ship with thousands of passengers. We both instinctively turned to look at an engraved presentation gold pan hanging on his wall. It commemorated the *Prinsendam* rescue.

The *Prinsendam* presentation Gold Pan in
District Seventeen Commander's office

A Merchant Vessel Safety Story; The Prinsendam Rescue
Fire onboard a Cruise Ship
A call came in to the Juneau Operations Center at 0058 (58 minutes past midnight Yukon Standard Time) on 4 October 1980.

Back then there were four time zones in Alaska. The 427-foot Holland American cruise ship, *Prinsendam* reported that they had an engine room fire.[1]

Their position was 150 miles west of Yakutat in the middle of the Gulf of Alaska. Their last port had been Ketchikan and they were heading for Unimak Pass on a great circle route to Singapore with 519 combined passengers and crew on board.[2] The great majority of the passengers were elderly tourists. At seven years old, the *Prinsendam* was the smallest, but newest of the Holland America fleet. Designed for intimate cruising with exotic destinations, she had 201 staterooms. Her crew consisted of Dutch Officers and mostly Indonesian crewmen. [3]

The ship's captain, Cornelius Wabeke was a thirty-year Holland American veteran. This morning he broadcast his first directed transmission of "XXX" alerting the world to a potential problem, but stating that the crew was successfully fighting the fire.[4]

Need Assistance

An hour later, at 0129 he reported the fire was burning out of control and sent out an SOS. The engineering department had evacuated the engine room in order to activate the CO_2 system with the hope of depriving the fire of oxygen, thereby snuffing it out. Prior to leaving the engine room, all the engines were shut down, which also secured the ships electrical generators, depriving the vessel of its electrical power and setting the ship adrift.[5] This was to have serious consequences as electrical power was needed for both the fire fighting pumps and the primary source of power for the boat davits. Davits are the structures with pulleys and lines

---

1   Schoel, M/V Prinsendam SAR Case Study, Executive Study

2   ibid

3   Josh Eppinger, *History's Greatest Sea Rescue*, (Popular Mechanics, April 1981), 102-105, 211-219

4   Jeffers, 76

5   ibid, 75

for lowering the lifeboats, which in this case had to be lowered seventy feet to the oceans surface.

Muster All Passengers

The Captain awakened the passengers with the sobering news that there was a fire in the engine room. He said it was under control but as a precaution he asked that they muster on the Promenade deck. This announcement, accompanied by the smell of smoke prompted the groggy, elderly passengers to report to their mustering stations in varying degrees of readiness. Some came dressed warmly with their lifejackets; some came in only their pajamas. The ship had held the mandatory emergency drills, required by the Coast Guard, three days earlier on 1 October. An abandon ship drill was held with all passengers required to attend with their lifejackets. They were all assigned to lifeboats at that time. An experienced passenger said the drill was efficient and impressive, with boats partially lowered.[6] However, like any drill, not everyone had taken it seriously. They were to wish they had, as the cold night, and hot fire, wore on.

Unlike the *Titanic*, which had lifeboats for less than half its passengers, the *Prinsendam* was well equipped for an emergency. She was constructed with ten watertight bulkheads containing twenty-five watertight doors. On the starboard or vessel's right side were two lifeboats each with a capacity of ninety-nine. Hanging from the davits was a forty-three person capacity motor launch. In addition there were six inflatable life rafts that could hold twenty-five persons each. On the port, or left side, were an additional six rafts, two lifeboats, and a motorized launch. Each motorized boat had a radio and all boats and rafts had survival equipment.[7]

Getting the Rescue Assets Moving

Back at Coast Guard headquarters in Juneau, Commander Dick Schoal, my predecessor as Chief of Search and Rescue, rushed in to the operations center on the seventh floor of the nine-story

---

6   Jeffers, 55

7   ibid, 48-9

Federal Building. He had raced in the twelve miles from his home in the Mendenhall Valley. Dick quickly assessed his assets and the situation. He requested a surface picture of merchant vessels in the area from the AMVER Center in New York. AMVER is an acronym that stands for automated mutual-assistance vessel rescue, and is a voluntary program started in 1958 in which merchant vessels report their position on a regular basis and are tracked by Coast Guard computers. Information such as if the vessel has a doctor on board is also available. An electronic surface picture, or SURPIC, with a prescribed radius around a disaster was possible in a matter of minutes. At this time in the 1980's over 2,000 ship position reports were received daily.

"Launch the Ready Aircraft – Fire on Cruise Ship"
Aircraft
The first rule in disaster assistance is "Get your assets moving." Commander Schoal directed air stations at Sitka, 170 nautical miles (NM) from on scene, and Kodiak, 250 NM away, to both launch helicopters and a C-130 respectively.

Canadian aviation resources in Comox, 600 NM away were requested from RCC Victoria, and the USAF Rescue Coordination Center at Elmendorf AFB in Anchorage was asked to assist.

Ships
The USCGC *Boutwell*, a 378-foot high endurance cutter, was in port in Juneau in conjunction with the Juneau Centennial Celebration. Juneau was approximately 300 miles from the *Princedom*'s position. Schoal directed the ship to do a recall of the crew on liberty and prepare to get underway. The Juneau police and fire departments were requested to help with rounding up the crew. The potential disaster's scope did not permit the *Boutwell* Captain, Lee Crumb, to wait for everyone to be located and a little over an hour from notification they were casting off the mooring lines. Several of the crew, including the #2 officer, the executive officer, T.D. Smith, were left behind. They were to miss an extraordinary rescue.

Likewise, the Buoy Tender *Woodrush* in port at Sitka was ordered to prepare to respond.

Responders On Scene

The first unit on scene at 0306 was an HH-3F helicopter CGNR 1472 from Sitka that was piloted by Lieutenant Commander Thuma. The crew reported on scene conditions as wind of ten knots, sea of ten feet, and unlimited visibility.[8] A C-130 from Kodiak piloted by Lieutenant Commander Barnstein, was overhead at 0320 and assumed On Scene Commander duties. This was standard operating procedure due to the C-130's enhanced endurance and communications capabilities.

"Now Hear This, Abandon Ship"

At 0512 the *Prinsendam*'s Captain determined that the situation was out of control and ordered the ship abandoned. By now the passengers had been milling around for four hours. They were no longer at their mustering stations, nor were they better equipped than when they left their warm staterooms, except for some who had pulled down curtains from the lounge to wrap themselves in.[9] One of the few unique aspects of that night was the appearance of unusually spectacular northern lights. The darkened ship probably added to the effect. However, it's doubtful that the passengers enjoyed the display.

Conditions Perilous

The situation was complicated and dangerous. They were in the middle of the Gulf of Alaska, in the dark, with extremely hypothermic conditions and hundreds of fragile, untrained and frightened souls. The outside air temperature was four degrees C or thirty-nine degrees F and it was very dark, with sunrise two hours away. As is often the case in Alaska, heavy weather was

---

8   ibid, Chronological Log

9   Jeffers. 158

coming as well. Typhoon Thelma had been born in mid-Pacific on 27 September and was moving toward the area.[10]

A Good Samaritan Joins the Party

An extremely fortunate circumstance was that the Tanker *Williamsburg*, fully loaded and outbound from Valdez, monitored the distress message. The giant 1000-foot super-tanker was ninety miles south of the *Prinsendam* destined for Texas with one and a half million barrels of crude. In the best traditions of mariners assisting one another she immediately came about and proceeded at her best speed of seventeen knots. This meant she would be on scene in approximately five and a half hours.

Evacuation Difficulties

The evacuation of the *Prinsendam* was not proceeding well. The starboard motor launch was lowered successfully, although manually as there was no electrical power. The port launch, however, became tangled up and was hanging at a 45-degree angle bow down. She was to remain thus for the duration. This meant that the remainder of the lifeboats had to carry more than their design capacity. Ninety persons crowded into a boat designed for sixty.

There were also reports of some of the Indonesian crew pushing ahead of the passengers into the boats. Passengers who ended up in the twenty-five person capacity covered rubber rafts soon found themselves sitting in a half a foot of water as they didn't know how to close the access door. They were alive however and off the burning ship. Most importantly, a lot of help was on the way.

The launching of the lifeboats and rafts was not pretty. One boat was being lowered on top of another, which could not clear the lowering apparatus. A disaster was averted only when a CG helicopter saw the dangerous situation and alerted the lowering party by flashing their searchlight at them. In all six lifeboats and four life rafts were successfully lowered. Approximately forty persons were left on board including fifteen passengers. The last

---

10   Jeffers, 34

boat lowered was at 0627. Sunrise was still over an hour away, and the *Williamsburg* was estimating to be on scene at 0745.

Help on the Way

The *Boutwell*, once clear of Gastineau Channel near Juneau, put her two turbines on line giving a top speed of nearly thirty knots. This meant she was burning 2,000 gallons of jet fuel an hour, but speed was of the essence.

The USAF H-3 escorted by its big brother C-130 also knew that getting on scene ASAP was critical. They elected to cut through Portage Pass, gambling that it would not be socked in by weather. At first it looked like they would lose the gamble. This time they and the evacuees were lucky. Thirty minutes after takeoff, the H-3 hit Portage Pass only to find it socked in with fog. After orbiting for a brief period the fog lifted sufficiently for the helicopter to slip through. The Air Force team had an advantage over the Coast Guard in that their H-3 was air refuelable from their big-brother C-130. This meant that as far as fuel was concerned, they could stay on scene indefinitely.

There were two specially trained Air Force rescue personnel known as Pararescue Jumpers or PJ's onboard the USAF helicopter. The lead PJ was Staff Sergeant John Cassidy, who was on his last alert in Alaska as he had orders to Korea. Onboard the escorting Air Force C-130 was a USAF doctor and three medical personnel in addition to the flight crew. These assets would prove invaluable in triaging the survivors once onboard the *Williamsburg*.

Standing By to Assist

By now there were several helicopters on scene in addition to the big 4-engine C-130 circling overhead. The initial decision was to await the arrival of the *Williamsburg* and allow them to recover the nearly 500 survivors in the small flotilla.

Hoisting from a small boat by helicopter is not a simple thing. The pilot has limited visibility below him. In the case of a life raft, he cannot see it at all once over it. He relies on the hoist operator to "Conn. me in" by giving him constant directions and information as to where the helicopter is in relationship to the hoisting area. Also the downwash from the eleven-ton whirly-bird is hurricane force and causes a blinding spray. This process requires constant practice and coordination between the pilot and hoist operator.

The hoisting device that the Coast Guard crews normally use is a rectangular welded metal basket at the end of a slim braided wire cable. The basket is affectionately known as the "baby carriage." The hydraulic hoist is capable of lifting up to 600 pounds at a time. In a pinch the basket can hold two people sitting down and has floats at either end. The floats allow a skilled hoist operator to scoop an unconscious person or object from the water. The crews practice constantly so that they can work effectively together.

The Coast Guard had no rescue swimmer program at the time. The flight crews of the H-3 helicopters consisted of a pilot and copilot forward and a hoist operator and radioman aft. The H-3 has a large cabin area and could accommodate a dozen or so survivors at a time. A normal rescue from a vessel would utilize communications between the helicopter and the boat operator to discus procedures, the best heading for the vessel to take to put the helicopter into the wind and procedures for handling the basket. None of this was possible with the *Prinsendam* survivors. There were no radios on the majority of the boats and none of the rafts. The great majority of the surface craft had no propulsion and were simply drifting. Most of the occupants of the boats and rafts were elderly, unfamiliar with procedures, and by now, wet and hypothermic.

The Air Force H-3 PJ's, in addition to being trained in rescue procedures, were also emergency medical technicians who could provide basic medical care. The two PJ's were put into the ocean and they swam to lifeboat number six. The Air Force rescue device was different as well. It was known as a "penetrator," and it could be lowered through heavy tree cover for jungle rescue. Three fold out legs were used for a trained person to sit on and to be hoisted into the helicopter. This device, unlike the Coast Guard basket, required training and familiarity to be used safely.

Fire Fighting Expert On Scene

The evacuees were next treated to a unique sight when a Sitka H-3 lowered a Coast Guard firefighting expert, Chief Warrant Officer Matz, to the *Prinsendam* along with pumps and hoses. The delivery was successful, but the success was short lived as the couplings on the CG equipment didn't match those of the ships. In the process of attempting to rig a solution, the pump slid over the side in the increasingly heavy seas.

Williamsburg On Scene

The *Williamsburg* came steaming up on scene at 0743, shortly after sunrise. It was a beautiful sight to the seasick survivors, but maneuvering the behemoth, as large as an aircraft carrier, around the little flotilla took great finesse. Even though the full crude load made her ride low in the water, it was still a forty-foot climb up the vertical ship's side.[11] The means of gaining the safety of the ship was a swaying rope ladder that had to be grabbed from a rocking boat, rising and falling as much as 15 feet with the passing seas. One passenger, Isabella Brex, a retired school nurse, successfully climbed the ladder to the deck of the *Williamsburg*.

It became apparent that the majority of the seniors, even in the best of times, couldn't mange, and in their near hypothermic state, this very physical feat was impossible. The only option until the *Boutwell* arrived was to start hoisting by helicopter.

Hoisting the Survivors

At 0835, H3 1472 began hoisting survivors, and fifteen minutes later it landed on the *Williamsburg* with the first eight. The 1472 crew continued hoisting and transferred two more loads of ten and twelve, respectively. The AF H3 802 began hoisting at 0940 bolstering the helicopter transfer. The helicopters would hoist up to a dozen survivors at a time and then fly to the *Williamsburg*. The helicopters would land at one of the two helicopter landing areas where crewmembers assisted the survivors in the long walk into the interior of the vessel's deckhouse. At that point, the Air

---

11   Jeffers, 208

Force and Canadian medical personnel, as well as the school nurse, Mrs. Brex, triaged and treated them.

They were all seasick and hypothermic and some were near death from exposure but there were no reported serious injuries. The Canadian medical personnel had been flown to Yakutat and were transferred to the *Williamsburg* by CG H3. At 1100 CG H3 1472 departed scene with seven survivors heading to Yakutat to offload survivors and refuel. They switched crews to meet crew rest requirement in Yakutat before returning to scene. At this time the original crew had done 110 hoists of survivors and must have been exhausted.

Prinsendam Abandoned

At 1315 the *Prinsendam* Captain reported the fire totally out of control and requested all persons be evacuated. Three helicopters were directed to proceed to the ship to take off the last forty persons. The USAF H3 was one of the helicopters that proceeded to the *Prinsendam* and recovered the remaining crew. By this time the helicopter had transferred forty-two of the sixty passengers from lifeboat number six. During this time one of the Canadian H-46 Labrador helicopters en route to the scene had a problem. They experienced an electrical fire and declared an emergency saying they were diverting to Yakutat. The Air Force C-130 left scene to escort the Canadian helicopter.

Air Force Helicopter Hits a Snag

Once the persons had been hoisted from the *Prinsendam* and flown to the *Williamsburg*, the Air Force H3 returned to lifeboat number 6 to finish recovering the survivors. The weather by now had gotten worse and swells over twenty feet were reported. In the process of lowering the penetrator, the cable became entangled under the lifeboat and was parted when the boat fell with the swell. Luckily no one was injured, but the helicopter was now out of the hoisting business. With her big brother C-130 having departed scene to escort the Canadian helicopter and now low on fuel the crew elected to land on the helicopter pad of a second tanker, the *Sohio Intrepid*, reporting on scene and to shut down. The helicopter was safely on board the ship at 1649.

Recovery of the survivors continued in a complex but professional ballet. Fresh helicopter crews were flown to Yakutat by C-130. Six different helicopters were utilized to hoist survivors. The *Boutwell* was also recovering survivors with its ship's motor launches. The *Boutwell* itself would maneuver along side a lifeboat and pull people onboard. In one instance, a middle-aged female passenger dressed only in her bathrobe was hoisted aboard. In the process her robe was blown off and she arrived on deck in only her birthday suit. She nevertheless grabbed the nearest Coastie and gave him a big hug.

Rescue Complete

By 1800, or thirteen hours after the order to abandon ship was given, the *Boutwell* reported that all the lifeboats and life rafts had been accounted for. The *Williamsburg* departed scene for Valdez, the *Boutwell* for Sitka and the aircraft for their various homes.

The actual headcount of the survivors was complicated. The *Williamsburg* had 350 persons on board. The Cutter *Boutwell* had recovered an additional eighty-four. In various helicopter trips to Yakutat for refueling, the helicopters had transferred sixty-two survivors directly from the lifeboats to land. At the time, however, exact counts were difficult given the numbers of units involved. In all there were four vessels, six helicopters, and three C-130s involved.

Many additional people assisted. Alaska State Troopers notified Rescue Coordination Center (RCC) Juneau that the local Yakutat disaster team had been activated and were bringing supplies to the airport. As word of the scope of the disaster spread many agencies and individuals offered assistance. RCC Elmendorf offered to fly food via USAF C130 to Yakutat. Also Valdez began making arrangement to receive the *Williamsburg* with its load of survivors. Alaska Airlines transferred blankets to Yakutat via one of their scheduled flights.

"Where's My PJ's?"
All seemed well as the rescue armada headed for home, but not so fast. At 1900, RCC Elmendorf contacted RCC Juneau asking, "Where are my PJs?" Juneau didn't know. The RCC contacted the *Boutwell*, *Williamsburg*, Yakutat and Sitka with no luck. By 2010 it was determined that there was a missing lifeboat with survivors onboard.

Back to the Scene
The *Boutwell* and *Woodrush* were directed to return to scene and commence a search. Conditions by now were terrible with visibility of less than a mile in blowing rain. The CGC *Woodrush* arrived on scene at 2240 and began an expanding square search pattern. Shortly after midnight a lookout on the *Woodrush* sighted a light and possibly a red flare. The *Boutwell* sped to the scene and located lifeboat number six with eighteen survivors and the missing two PJ's. The *Boutwell* recovered the survivors in a little over an hour and departed for Sitka.

The Survivors Ashore.
Boutwell arrived in Sitka with eighty-seven survivors at 1600 local on 5 October, approximately thirty-five hours after the *Prinsendam* was abandoned. The *Williamsburg* arrived in Valdez three hours later with 370 rescuees. A total of sixty-two others had been transferred ashore by various helicopters to Yakutat and Sitka. The total was 519. All were finally accounted for. At Sitka, Valdez and Yakutat the local citizens turned out in great numbers to welcome the survivors and provide them with clothing, hot food, a cold drink or two, and a warm hug.

Prinsendam sinking in the Gulf of Alaska

Attempting to Save the Ship

Later, the *Prinsendam* was taken in tow by a commercial tug with the hope of making it to a repair facility in the lower 48. The fires continued, however, ultimately melting many portholes and much superstructure, allowing the vessel to take on more and more water. Finally the gallant lady could take no more and she sank on 11 October. Despite the loss of the vessel, this was the most successful sea rescue of all time. It was truly an international and inter-service team effort. At various times it involved two high endurance cutters, the *Boutwell* and *Mellon*, the Buoy Tender *Woodrush*, two H-3 helicopters from Kodiak, two H-3s from Sitka, two C-130s from Kodiak, Two H-46 Canadian helicopters, two Buffaloes and one Argus fixed wing aircraft and an H-3 and C-130 from Elmendorf Air Force Base. In addition, the communities of Yakutat, Sitka, Valdez and Juneau all pitched in to help.

This was also possibly the most decorated rescue of all time. Recommendations were submitted for thirteen Distinguished Flying Crosses, seven Air Medals, eight Meritorious Service Medals, twenty-two Coast Guard Commendation Medals, five Coast Guard Achievement Medals, thirty-four Coast Guard

Letters of Commendation and twelve Unit Commendations. Richly deserved I might add. I'm sure the passengers and crew of the *Prinsendam* would agree.[12]

Why Does the Coast Guard do Merchant Vessel Safety?
Background
The marriage of the steam engine and the ship was a good thing. It gave a reliable source of propulsion regardless of the wind. There was just one problem. The touchy boilers would often blow up with catastrophic results. Up to 1832, explosions or fire destroyed fourteen percent of vessels built with steam propulsion. The worst case involved the Mississippi River steamboat *Sultana*. An explosion of three of its four boilers on 27 April 1865 resulted in the worst maritime disaster in U. S. history, with an estimated loss of 1,800 lives.[13]

In reaction to public pressure Congress passed laws in a patchwork way to fix the problems without severely taxing the industry with expenses. Congress was reluctant to impede the growing steamboat industry, which was playing a significant role in the nation's economic growth.

Merchant Vessel Safety's mission started with the Steamboat Inspection Service that was established by Congress in 1838 in the Justice Department. It was apparently placed in this unlikely bureaucratic home to have the enforcement capability. In 1884 the Bureau of Navigation was established also in Treasury along with the Revenue Cutter Service.

MVS Laws
The latter part of the 1840's saw numerous boiler and other disasters, again prompting a public outcry. Congress reacted with The *Steamboat Act of May 30, 1852*, again in Treasury. This act established nine supervisory inspector positions responsible for separate geographic areas. Important provisions of this act were a

---

12   Schoel, Military Award Recommendations

13   Wikipedia, *SS Sultana*

requirement for hydrostatic testing of boilers and the installation of boiler safety valves. The law further required the licensing of pilots and engineers of the vessels. Once again politics limited the scope of the legislation by exempting freight boats, ferries, tugboats and towboats.[14]

The Steamboat Inspection Service was created by an act of Congress passed on 28 February 1871. This important act remedied some of the ills of the prior legislation and created a comprehensive marine safety code. It also required licensing all masters and chief mates. The next ingredient in this recipe occurred when Congress enacted *Public Law 622*, which transferred the Steamboat Inspection Service to the newly created Department of Commerce and Labor. The Bureau of Navigation, which had been created in 1884, was merged into the organization to oversee the regulation of merchant marine seaman. The name of this new combination of functions was changed to the Bureau of Marine Inspection and Navigation, still within the Department of Commerce. An important responsibility of the new organization was a requirement that the Bureau approve all passenger vessel plans before a vessel was constructed.

The last responsibility added was the *Motorboat Act of 1940*. This specified safety requirements for every vessel propelled by machinery not more that 65-feet in length and set requirement for safety equipment and running lights. It also spelled out procedures for reckless or negligent operations. This was the beginning of the Coast Guard Boating Safety mission.[15]

Let the Coast Guard Do It

This complex bag of responsibilities was handed to the Coast Guard by executive order signed by President Roosevelt in 1942, which transferred the Bureau of Marine Inspection and Navigation temporarily as a wartime measure. The transfer

---

14   USCG Missions Timeline, *Marine Safety*, (Washington D.C., USCG History Program) 6

15   ibid, 7

became permanent with the *Reorganization Plan Number 3* on 16 July 1946.

An important addition to this litany of responsibilities was the *Small Passenger Vessel Act of May 10, 1956*. This law required all vessels carrying six or more persons for hire to comply with a number of requirements including: possessing lifesaving and fire fighting equipment as well as machinery and electrical installation, hull strength and stability considerations. It further specified licensing of all operators and set manning standards.

The fishing vessel industry got a big safety boost when President Reagan signed into law the *Commercial Fishing Industry Vessel Safety Act*. Amazingly enough this was the first safety legislation earmarked specifically for commercial fishing vessels. This mixed bag of responsibilities belongs to the Coast Guard, with their program managers being the Marine Safety Offices (MSOs) who often wear several hats as Marine Inspectors and Captain of the Ports. A new responsible office, established by Congress, was the Coast Guard's Passenger Vessel Safety Program, which was established in each Coast Guard District office and in Sector San Juan.

Marine Safety in Alaska

Alaska again is different. There are minimal shipyards, and even the state ferries go outside for their maintenance. So the approval of plans and monitoring of vessel construction is minimal. Cruise ships on the other hand are very much big business for Alaska. Cruise ships brought one million passengers in 2008. This is more people than live in Alaska (722,718 estimate for July 2011 as per the U.S. Census Bureau).

Who's In Charge?

Alaska's Marine Safety program is divided into three Marine Inspection Zones and Captain of the Port Zones, which are managed by Marine Safety Office (MSO) Southeast (Juneau), Western Alaska (Anchorage) and Prince Williams Sound (Valdez). There have been marine safety detachments in Dutch Harbor, Sitka, Kenai, Ketchikan, and Kodiak. The goal of marine safety is prevention. Remembering the *Prinsendam*'s abandon ship problems, the marine safety offices periodically require cruise ships to lower their lifeboats, and now every cruise begins sometime in the first day or two with an abandon ship drill for all passengers.

Fishing vessels in Alaska are dangerous places to work. You only need to watch the "Deadliest Catch" to see why. The marine safety offices enforce the *Commercial Vessel Safety Act* that became law in 1992 and have substantially reduced the number of fatalities on fishing vessels. To accomplish this, over 1,000 dockside inspections are conducted annually in Alaska by a team of active duty Coast Guard personnel and Coast Guard Auxiliarists.

The marine safety offices also are charged with investigating marine casualties within Alaskan waters. These can be very difficult to accomplish when the incident occurs on some remote island in the Aleutians in the dead of winter. In summary this is a very important and complex mission. The dedicated professionals in Marine Safety don't get the medals that their flying counterparts do, but they definitely save lives and protect the environment as unsung heroes.

Chapter Thirteen

Boating Safety

Boating safety is a bread and butter mission for the Coast Guard with over twelve million registered recreational vessels in the United States. Alaska alone had 48,891 recreational vessels in 2010. Education and emphasis on accident prevention must be stressed with that many boaters

A Boating Safety Story - The Raspberry Island Deer Hunt

It was an ideal deer-hunting day at first light. Mike Stenger and I, along with three other pilots, were trailering our nineteen-foot Dorsett boat across the mountain to Anton Larson Bay to launch. Mike and I, along with Jim "Frannie" Wright were co-owners of this boat on a sort of time-share arrangement. Not having much money back in those days, we jointly were able to afford a much better boat than if we had to buy one alone.

The Hunt Plan

We planned to motor across Kizhuyak Bay, through Whale Pass, and anchor in a bay at Raspberry Island. The twelve-mile drive over the mountains to Anton Larsen was uneventful. We went by Pyramid Mountain at the halfway point and soon after had a panoramic view of Anton Larsen Bay. We launched our nineteen-foot inboard/outboard and headed to Raspberry. The seas were calm with little wind. It was in the 30's, barely above freezing but we were all dressed for it and enjoyed the cold crisp air.

Once we got to Raspberry we dropped everyone off. Mike anchored the boat and used the dinghy, which we had been towing, to come ashore. The five of us discussed when to return and then split into two parties. We started climbing to higher ground where we thought the deer would be feeding or bunked down.

Daughter Nicole and Kathleen Stenger with Kodiak crab and our Dorsett in the background

The Weather Changes
After a couple of hours we noticed things beginning to change fast. I remember thinking that the clouds were like one of those old Walt Disney time-lapse nature films when stuff moves super fast. The clouds began building and moving rapidly across the sky with increasing wind. This weather was unexpected and un-forecasted, which was not unusual for Kodiak in those days before satellites.

We all started heading down towards the beach as the wind began picking up, and rain mixed with sleet began pelting us.

Back near where we started, there was a cabin with a nice old guy and his girlfriend. He said "You boys better hole up with me until this blows over." Where we were anchored was just off Raspberry Straits, which was somewhat protected from the wind and eventually led into Kizhuyak Bay' From there it was five miles of open water to cross to the entrance to Anton Larsen Bay. Mike said, "Why don't we go down the Straits and see what Kizhuyak is like. If it's too rough we'll come back." After some mumbling and muttering we agreed to try it.

Mike rowed the dinghy back out to the boat, however he was unable to pull up the anchor because of the force of the wind, so he cut the anchor line. This should have been our first red flag. We, however, stuck with the original plan and all boarded our little cabin cruiser. By now the wind was a constant twenty-five knots (28.8 MPH) with gusts to thirty-five knots. This should have been the second red flag.

Swells Too Big to Come About
When we hit the mouth of Raspberry Straits we immediately were in ten-foot wind-driven swells, and the wind was gusting even higher than before. By now our fellow travelers were all seasick, lying in the cabin and basically useless. Mike and I did a quick assessment. He said, "I'm afraid to try and come about (turn around) in these seas, and I think we can make it." Together we plotted a line on the chart and using our little wet compass about the size of a grapefruit we headed for the entrance to Anton Larsen. Visibility was now about 100 yards in sleet that was freezing on the windshield. Mike had to lean out the side to see ahead. We were starting to take on water, with wind blown water crashing over the bow and windward sides. The dinghy that we were towing was airborne half the time as it rolled up and down the swells.

Taking on Water
Mike shouted, "Don't let the engine flood out!" Our inboard engine was in a low well and the water from the heavy rain and

waves breaking over us was flowing into the well. I quickly got our hand held bilge pump and began shooting the water over the side in squirts. Because of the size of the swells we were only able to make a couple of knots of forward speed. I was beginning to worry that we were burning a lot of our gas and not making much progress. Mike kept steering the heading as best he could but we had no idea how much the wind was blowing us off our desired track. Our three friends were contemplating shooting either themselves or us. This went on forever, but it was probably only an hour when God once again protected the ignorant.

Anton Larsen Entrance

Looming out of the sleet and snow was the entrance to Anton Larsen dead on. With a shout for joy I turned the bilge pump squirts on Mike who was so wet by now he didn't even notice. After securing our sturdy little boat on its trailer we decided the roads over the mountain pass would be too slick to try and tow it so we left it for the next day and drove back to the base.

When we got to our quarters, both wives said, "What the f**k are you doing here?" It seems they had called the operations officer when the weather turned lousy and he assured them "Oh, these guys are experienced pilots, they'll hole up till it blows over." Which means of course that if we had capsized, they probably wouldn't have come looking for us until long after we were frozen dead.

"Tell 'Em How Stupid You Were"

The final well deserved humiliation came because I was the senior man in the whole debacle. At the next pilot's meeting, Captain Nelson, the CO, made me explain what a stupid thing we had done and to advise the other officers to never do the same thing. The similarities to this story and the crash of the C-130 on Attu should be obvious. An experienced crew, thinking they can handle anything nature can throw their way, is proven wrong. It boils down to chance, one crew survived their stupidity and one did not.

Why is the Coast Guard Involved with Boating Safety?

The Laws

Congress passed the *Motorboat Act of 1910* and gave the Revenue Cutter Service responsibility to enforce it. This tasking was increased by the *Federal Boat Safety Act of 1971.*

Mission Scope

The size of the Boating Safety, or "B" programs is impressive. In 2010 there were 12,438,926 boats registered. These boats had a total of 4,604 accidents with 672 fatalities, 3,153 injured and damages over $35 million.[1] To reduce the chance for injury to the seventy-seven million adults that engage in recreational boating, the Coast Guard develops and enforces vessel construction and performance standards. Enforcing the standards requires inspection of approximately 2,000 recreational boat manufacturers annually. Both active duty and auxiliary members annually accomplish a boarding program of over a million boardings'.[2]

Auxiliary is a Big Help

All of this could not be done without the assistance of the volunteer arm of the Coast Guard family, the Auxiliary. These dedicated 32,000 men and women purchase their own uniforms and provide 5,000 operational vessels, over 200 aircraft and several thousand-communication stations. Equally important is the safe boating instruction they provide the public, and their assistance with safety patrol hours and over a quarter of a million hours in mission support.

How does the Coast Guard do Boating Safety in Alaska?

U. S. boating safety statistics are kept for fifty-six areas, which include the fifty states plus American Samoa, District of Columbia,

---

1   *Recreational Boating Statistics 2010,* (COMDTINST P19754.24, 13 June 2011) 53, 65

2   Coast Guard Budget Document 2008, 21

Guam, Northern Marianas Island, Puerto Rico and the Virgin Islands. Of these fifty-six areas Alaska ranks forty-sixth in the numbers of registered vessel. This is still nearly 49,000 vessels. For 2010 in Alaska there were eight fatalities and damage to property of $753,675.[3] Just as in the national picture education and prevention are the emphasis. The Auxiliary is of great assistance in this effort in the Last Frontier with 400 members in flotillas in Juneau, Ketchikan, Kodiak, Whittier Seward and Anchorage.

---

3   Recreational Boating Statistics, 65 & 53.

Chapter Fourteen

Cooperation with Other Agencies (COOP)

Lesser Canadian Geese are established on Kodiak Island in
a cooperative program with Alaska Fish and Game

COOP, Not a Place to Keep Chickens

Cooperating with other agencies in performing their official duties isn't really a specified Coast Guard mission. However, Coast Guard units can, and do, assist other agencies and governmental bodies.

This was the flight code we would use when we would do some of these odd missions. These flights were always highly sought after among the pilots because of their uniqueness. Some of the fun missions I did included assisting the Alaska State Division of Fish and Game in establishing lesser Canadian geese on Kodiak Island, doing bear surveys, looking for marijuana farms in Oregon forests, even an aerial search for a bank robbers get-away car.

In the early days in Alaska, the Revenue Cutters were critical in transporting public health personnel, judges, law enforcement officials, census takers and the list is endless. One of the most interesting and important relationships was between a Presbyterian missionary named Shelton Jackson, and the infamous skipper "Hell-roaring" Mike Healy of the Cutter *Bear*.

A Coop Story - The Overland Expedition

The Native School reindeer herds played an important role in one of the most bizarre but heroic Coast Guard rescues of all times.

The Background

In the last week of September of 1897, eight whaling ships were trapped off Point Barrow with an early onset of the ice. The plight of the ships was learned from one of their sister ships, the *Karluk*, that had managed to break out before being trapped.[1] Once word of the potential tragedy reached the San Francisco newspapers they quickly took up the cry, including one headline, "Crews of Whaling Vessels Ice-Bound in the Arctic Have No Hope of Rescue." Telegrams were sent to President McKinley to do something. The President turned to his Treasury Secretary Lyman J. Gage. Gage in turn asked Rev. Jackson for his recommendations. His answer – Reindeer.

SAR - Eight Vessels Trapped in Ice. Crews Starving.

An urgent letter, dated 15 November 1897, was sent from Gage to Captain Francis Tuttle who had relieved Healy as skipper of the *Bear*. The *Bear* had just returned to Seattle three weeks prior, after six

---

1   Paul H. Johnson, *The Overland Expedition: A Coast Guard Triumph*, (New London, CT, Coast Guard Academy Alumni Association Bulletin, September 1972) 63-71

hard months in the Arctic. The ten-page letter spelled out in great detail that a rescue mission involving driving reindeer to Barrow should be attempted. I suspect that Dr. Jackson drafted the letter for the Secretary of the Treasury's signature, as it mentioned many missionary and Alaskan native herders by name, as well as the size of their reindeer herds.[2] As instructed, Captain Tuttle asked for volunteers to attempt the mission and had no trouble filling out the crew.

The Mission

Crew of the R/C Bear; Captain Tuttle, center front row, Lieutenant Jarvis on Tuttle's right Berthoff is far left, front row

After outfitting the *Bear*, Tuttle and his crew sailed from Seattle and arrived at Dutch Harbor on 9 December. There they took on coal and supplies that included additional dogs and sleds, and Tuttle posted a letter back to Secretary Gage of their progress. The *Bear* sailed in a snowstorm at 0135 on 11 December.[3]

---

2   L.J. Gage, Secretary of the Treasury, *Letter of Instruction to Captain Francis Tuttle, R.C.S.*, (Washington D.C., 15 November 1897)

3   F. Tuttle, Captain R.C.S., *Letter to Secretary of the Treasury*, (Dutch Harbor, Alaska, 23 December 1897)

Secretary Gage's detailed instruction had specified sailing to Norton Sound to put the party ashore. The Arctic had other ideas. The same conditions that had trapped the whalers now presented the *Bear* with ice conditions much worse and much further south than expected. Tuttle was forced to put the relief party ashore near Cape Vancouver, which was 700 miles south of the desired starting point.

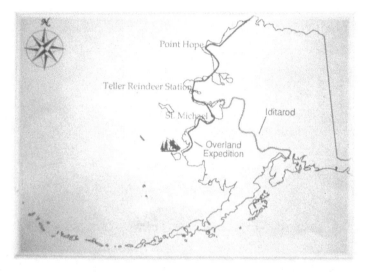

Overland expedition route, nearly 1,500 miles

Remembering the picture of Alaska superimposed on the lower 48, the starting point would have been in northern New Mexico. They had to walk to Point Barrow, which again on our map would be on the Canadian U.S. Border. Also not to forget, this was December in the Arctic, and the last third of the trip would be north of the Arctic Circle, with no sun.

The Overland Rescue Principals

The three principals in this great adventure were well suited for their seemingly impossible task. The leader of the expedition was 1st LT David Jarvis, top man in his academy class of 1883. Jarvis was an eight-year Arctic veteran and was fluent in the Eskimo language. He was at the time the Executive Officer of the *Bear*.

Members of the *Bear* crew in the Overland Expedition. First Lieutenant Berthoff on left, Surgeon Call middle, and Lieutenant Jarvis

At left in the picture is the number two man, 2nd LT Ellsworth Berthoff. He was later to become the first Commandant of the U.S. Coast Guard, formed from combining the Revenue Cutter Service and the Lifesaving Service in 1915. The third member was Dr. Samuel J. Call, the ship's surgeon. The Doctor had five years of experience in Alaska working for the Alaska Commercial Company as their surgeon at Unalaska prior to joining the Revenue Cutter Service.

The Rescue Trek Begins

The *Bear* putting the party, their supplies, dogs and sleds ashore was a very dangerous operation. High winds and ice floes nearly sank the boats. The *Bear* couldn't get close to the shore because of the shallow water. Finally, by dusk the party was ashore and underway on its 1,500-mile odyssey. Included in the nearly 1,300 pounds of supplies were two bags of mail weighing seventy-five pounds destined for St Michael and Barrow.[4] Over the next one hundred days they were to endure temperatures as low as -60

---

4   First Lieutenant D. H. Jarvis, *Overland Relief Expedition report,* (Point Barrow, Alaska, 10 July, 1898)

degrees F, blizzards after blizzards, and the challenges of herding reindeer.

Help Along the Way

They were to get help from the Alaskan Natives along the way. Charlie Artisarlook donated 138 reindeer from his herd at Cape Prince of Wales. The missionary Tom Lopp was to do even better. Surely the unsung hero of the expedition, Lopp not only helped round up an additional 310 reindeer, but he agreed to join the team and assist with driving the herd north. This meant he had to leave his wife, Ellen, and four children, including a newborn, for many months in a Native village at Cape Prince of Wales.[5]

Jarvis arrived at Lopp's mission house on 24 January. They were still 700 miles away from Barrow. They were to persevere, however, and for the next unimaginable two months they trudged on. Finally, on 26 March 1898, they reached the southernmost of the trapped ships with 382 reindeer accompanying them.[6]

The reindeer meat was important but equally so was the discipline and order that Jarvis brought. He directed the building of additional shelters to ease the cramped and unsanitary conditions existing prior to their arrival. Jarvis also organized baseball games when weather permitted, so the survivors could get some exercise and recreation.

Success and Reward

The *Bear* finally broke through to Barrow on 28 July, not knowing what they were to find. Tuttle was delighted to learn that the project had been a great success and no whalers had been lost once Jarvis and Call had arrived. Loaded with survivors, the *Bear* arrived in Seattle on 13 September. They'd been gone ten months.

---

5   Taliaferro, *In a Far Country*, 239

6   Murry Lundberg, *Dr. Samuel J. Call in the Arctic Seas*, (Explore North, http://explorenorth.com/library/yafeatures/bi-DrCall.htm) 2

Recognition for the Overland Expedition. Better Late than Never

As an important footnote, Jarvis, Berthoff, and Call all received Congressional gold medals presented four years after the rescue.

Why Does the Coast Guard Cooperate with Other Agencies?

Cooperation with other agencies is something at which the Coast Guard has always excelled. After Katrina there was a famous Time Magazine Cover asking, "Why does the Coast Guard Get it Right, When Everyone Else Gets it Wrong?" I'm not sure we always get it right, but the Service has always stressed standardization and cooperation with others for the benefit of the nation. From the Revenue Cutter Service, to training foreign Coast Guards, to working with Alaska State Troopers to rescue stranded hunters, its what we do. Its what we've always done. Hopefully it's what we'll always do.

Chapter Fifteen

Fun & Games in Alaska

What brought my family and me back to Alaska so many times was the beauty and opportunities for adventure that it offers. My son Brad and his wife are still there. Brad at nearly 40 years of age, has lived in Alaska for all but eleven of those years because he loves it. Many people have a mental image of Alaska as a land of igloos, polar bears and danger. My memoir may have reinforced this with all the stories of disasters, earthquakes and dramatic rescues. In this final chapter I want to leave you with an appreciation of the attraction of Alaska, especially if you enjoy the outdoors.

Alaska Challenges and Myths

The first myth to dispel is that Alaska is a world of ice and cold. You have to keep in mind once more the scope of the place. It's different in all parts of the state due to its size, the fact that it's home to three major mountain ranges and the maritime influences. The weather in Ketchikan in Southeast Alaska is dramatically different than that of Barrow. In January, the average temperature in Ketchikan is thirty-four degrees Fahrenheit and the precipitation average is fourteen inches. In Barrow in January the average temperature is minus thirteen degrees Fahrenheit with 0.2 inches of precipitation. In August, Barrow averages thirty-seven degrees with less than an inch of rain while Ketchikan is fifty-eight degrees average with nearly eleven inches of rain for the month! The annual numbers show Barrow with 4.67 inches of rain and Ketchikan with 155 inches, or nearly thirteen feet of rain.[1] The twelve years we spent in Juneau were not unlike Seattle weather, except a few degrees colder with more snow than rain in the winter.

I want to be truthful, however. Winds are more of a factor than in most other places. We spoke earlier of the williwaw phenomena. Below are two pictures of flying approaches into Kodiak, one with wind and one without.

Good Kodiak

I took this picture on approach to the runway at Kodiak in a helicopter. The Coast Guard Base is to the left with Old Woman Mountain behind it. The town of Kodiak is off camera about six miles to the right.

---

1   Alaska Almanac, 32nd Edition, 50-51

Bad Kodiak

Here is what the flight picture looked like when Kodiak was blowing. Note Barometer Mountain at the end of the runway. (This was why you did not go past the missed approach point in a low visibility situation.) Wreckage of a Navy patrol plane and an USAF fighter on the mountain bore grim testimony for the unwary.

Alaska is a wonderful place for raising a family if you enjoy nature, regardless of the weather challenges. We had some great picnics with our friends and their kids. Our kids got to see things that most only read about in books. Our first memorable picnic took place with our sponsors on the beach in the cold with snow showers. When I had awakened that morning and seen the snow, I called my sponsor assuming the picnic was called off. "Negative!" he said "We don't let weather get in the way of a party in Alaska." Brad was seven months old and had a great time, snuggled in my flight parka on the beach, perfectly warm.

During another outing exploring a small offshore island, we found seagull nests that were laid on the beach where eggs were hatching. Daughter Nicole, in particular, was always fascinated with wildlife. She enjoyed seeing what made animals tick and even helped me skin out a black bear at one point. The hunting, fishing and crabbing were like nowhere else.

When we were stationed at Kodiak there was a shack at Old Woman's Bay that contained two gigantic steam cookers. These were about four feet high and could hold 20-30 crabs each. There was also a nice metal cleaning table with running water and a chute for the shell and waste to slide down into the bay where other crabs were waiting to scavenge it.

Nicole and Sasha with Kodiak crabs

Alaska the Beautiful

Flying helicopters on a daily basis gave me an opportunity to see spectacular places, great animals and challenging events. We were careful not to harass the wildlife, but it was fun to find them. I was especially fond of an elk herd on Afognak Island that was particularly elusive. The elk had been transplanted there from the Olympic Mountain range in Washington State some years ago and had taken well to their new home. Other animals we often saw were Sitka Black Tail deer, Dall Sheep, Rocky Mountain Goats, whales, sea lions and caribou. But the most awe inspiring of all was the Kodiak bear.

Large Kodiak bear on Afognak Island

This particular bear pictured was one of the largest I'd ever seen. He was very unconcerned about the helicopter. The relative size can be judged by comparing him to the trees. Bears are generally not a problem, but you should never take them for granted. The safety rules were never surprise a bear, make lots of noise so they know you're around and avoid bears with cubs and food. There's an old saying that only one bear in 20 is dangerous, but unfortunately they don't wear numbers.

A family favorite was to climb Old Woman Mountain behind the base at Kodiak. During certain times of the summer wild flowers grew in vast profusion there. Daughters Nicole and Sasha at one time tried to see how many different types of flowers they could find and, as I recall, they located over 40 different varieties.

Nicole and friends on Old Woman Mountain with
the Kodiak Base in the background

We did a lot of scary things with helicopters, but we also had
fun. One annual event that we all looked forward to was flying
Santa to the native villages on Kodiak. All year we would collect
one-pound coffee cans, which around Christmas would be filled
with home made cookies and candies by the various wives' clubs.
We would then fly to the ten or so villages around the island and
pass them out to the children with Santa doing the honors.

Flying Santa to the villages

Alaska, A Hunter's Delight

I was fortunate in that I hooked up with Mike Stenger, who checked into Kodiak with his family a week after we did in December 1973. Mike was one year behind me at the Academy, graduating in 1964. He had been prior enlisted and entered the Academy already a Petty Officer First Class. Except for the times when he tried to kill me with weather, he and I had exceptionally good luck in getting what we were stalking. Mike was an avid hunter and had been stationed in Alaska prior. I was somewhat of a novice. Mike helped me pick out a good all-round rifle (Remington BDL 30-06 with a 4 power Weaver scope). With that gun I was able to take a Dall sheep in the Talkeetna Mountains, a Rocky Mountain goat at Icy Bay Alaska, a brown bear at Yakutat, a black bear on Douglas Island, a caribou on the Alaska Peninsula and many deer in Southeast Alaska and on Kodiak.

Mike Stenger on the top of Barometer Mountain during
a hike with me to get in shape for sheep hunting.

Hunting in Alaska was not only fun but provided some delicious eating. The family favorite was Dall sheep. This was nothing like mutton or lamb in flavor. These sheep are large, very athletic animals. Their meat is fine-grained and very lean. A freezer is a must if you hunt in Alaska. We unfortunately received orders from Kodiak six months earlier than expected requiring us to depart just before Christmas in 1975 to attend the Armed Forces Staff College in Norfolk Virginia. These were great orders, but we had a freezer full of about 200 pounds of sheep, goat, deer and moose that we had to give away to neighbors.

Unique Opportunities

Another unique opportunity in much of Southeast and South-central Alaska is provided by the ferry system, known as the Alaska Marine Highway. In the Southeast a fleet of seven ferries provides scheduled service between Bellingham Washington and Prince Rupert, British Columbia, as well as many Southeast Alaska ports year round. When we lived in Juneau it was a nice weekend trip to sail to Sitka, visit the historic totem park, have lunch and then return. All very reasonably priced, and the trip itself was beautiful, sometimes punctuated with whales, wildlife, and vistas. In the winter, we would take our car on the ferry to Haines and drive up to see the Chilkat eagle gathering and visit friends. The Chilkat River was the last to freeze and the eagles would gather there in the thousands to partake of the late salmon runs.

Alaska State Department of Natural Resources (DNR)

Following retirement from the Coast Guard, I joined my wife Sylvia in employment with the State. The Department of Natural Resources (DNR) hired me, first as an Assistant Director of Administrative Services and later as the Executive Director of the Soil and Water Board.

Shortly after beginning with DNR, Sylvia was diagnosed with Non-Hodgkin's Lymphoma and had to go to Seattle for several months of treatment. I went with her. I had almost no sick leave at the time and barely knew anyone in the Department outside my immediate office. Nevertheless, the union voluntarily collected donated sick leave from our fellow workers to cover the time we were both absent during Sylvia's treatment. I was absolutely blown away by everyone's kindness. Alaskan's are an independent lot but they have a big heart.

In all I spent four tours in the Great Land, one on the icebreaker and three with the family. If I had to do it again I'd start even earlier trying to get orders there. I unfortunately listened to older officers who either had bad experiences in Alaska or had misgivings based on erroneous information. Once I saw Alaska I fell in love, and my family did as well. The fourth time we came back the whole family voted for it.

Eighth floor of the State Office Building (SOB) where Sylvia worked in Juneau. Note man in far left corner and size of Kodiak bear

Alaska is an important place. The Coast Guard has serious work there. Despite its challenges, I count myself as an Alaskan Guardian who considers it one of my favorite places on earth. I hope you've enjoyed my stories.

BIBLIOGRAPHY

Alaska Economic Trends, (Juneau, Alaska Department of labor and Workforce Development). Various months 2011.

Beard, Tom Editor-in-Chief. *The Coast Guard.* Seattle WA. Hugh Lauther Levin Associates, Inc. 2004.

Borneman, Walter R. *Alaska, Saga of a Bold Land.* New York. Harper Collins Publishers Inc. 2003.

Cohen, Stan. *The Great Alaska Pipeline.* Missoula, Montana. Pictorial Histories Publishing Co. 1988.

Cohen, Stan. *8.6 The Great Alaska Earthquake.* Missoula, Montana. Pictorial Histories Publishing Co. 1995.

Cohen, Stan. *The Streets Were Paved With Gold.* Missoula, Montana. Pictorial Histories Publishing Co. 1977.

Cohen, Stan. *The Forgotten War.* Missoula, Montana. Pictorial Histories Publishing Co. 1981.

Costello, John. *Days of Infamy.* New York. Pocket Books. 1994.

Davidson, Art. *In the Wake of the Exxon Valdez.* San Francisco, CA. Sierra Club Books. 1990.

Ferrell, Nancy Warren. *Alaska's Heroes, A Call to Courage*. Portland OR. Alaska Northwest Books. 2002

Gates, Nancy Editor. *The Alaska Almanac, Facts about Alaska 32nd Edition*. Portland Oregon. Alaska Northwest Books. 2008.

Garfield, Brian. *The Thousand-Mile War*. New York, NY. Bantam Books. 1988.

Helvarg, David. *Rescue Warrior*. New York. Thomas Dunne Books, St. Martin's Press. 2009.

Jeffers, H. Paul. *Burning Cold*. St. Paul, MN. Zenith Press. 2006.

Kaplan, H. R. and Hunt, James F., LCDR. USCG. *This is the Coast Guard*. Cambridge, MD. Cornell Maritime Press Inc. 1972.

Kroll, C. Douglas. *Commodore Ellsworth P. Bertholf*. Annapolis, Maryland. Naval Institute Press. 2002.

Laguardia-Kotite, Martha J. *So Others May Live*. Guilford CT. The Lyons press. 2006.

Lebedoff, David. *Cleaning up*. New York, NY. The Free Press. 1997

Noble, Dennis L *Alaska and Hawaii, A Brief History of Coast Guard Operations*, (Washington D.C., Coast Guard historians Office, 1991), 15-6

Noble, Dennis L. and Strobridge, Truman R. *Captain "Hell Roaring" Mike Healy*. Gainesville FL. University Press of Florida. 2009.

Prange, George W. *At Dawn We Slept*. New York. McGraw-Hill Book Company. 1981

Reeves, R. J. Lieutenant General, USAF. *Operation Helping Hand.* Anchorage, Headquarters Alaska Command. 1964

Rigge, Simon. *War In The Outposts.* Alexandria, Virginia. Time-Life Books.1980

Schoel, Richard L. CDR USCG, *M/V Prinsendam SAR Case Study,* Juneau Alaska, CCGD17 (osr)

Skinner, Samuel K. and Reilly, William K. *The Exxon Valdez Oil Spill.* Washington D.C., National Response Team, May 1989,

Strobridge, Truman R. and Noble, Dennis L *Alaska and the U.S. Revenue Cutter Service 1867-1915.* Annapolis, Maryland. Naval Institute Press. 1999.

Taliaerro, John. *In A Far Country.* New York, NY. Public Affairs Books. 2006.

Glossary

ATON – Aids to navigation.

Beam – The dimension of the width of a vessel at its broadest point.

C-130 – Four engine cargo plane known as Hercules and made by Lockheed.

Chain of Command – An organizational structure based on seniority in which the senior in the chain determines courses of actions or delegates it to those juniors in the chain.

COTP – Captain of the Port.

COOP – Cooperation with other agencies.

Cutter – Term for Cost Guard ships larger than boats. Refers back to Revenue Cutter Service started by Alexander Hamilton.

DEC – State of Alaska Department of Environmental Conservation.

Deck – A term for the floor of a boat. Also used to describe a floor of a building.

DFC – Distinguished Flying Cross. A senior award for heroism involving flight operations.

D-17 – The 17th Coast Guard District, which encompasses Alaska and its waters.

DOD – Department of Defense. The executive home of the Army, Air Force, Navy and Marines.

EEZ- Exclusive Economic Zone. 200 mile limit.

ELT - Enforcement of Laws and Treaties.

Flight Deck – Stern area of a Coast Guard Cutter or other vessel where takeoffs and landings are accomplished.

FCMA – *Fisheries Conservation and Management Act*, 200 mile limit.

FOSC – Federal On Scene Coordinator

H-3 – Large twin turbine helicopter named the Pelican made by Sikorsky and flown by the Coast Guard. Now retired.

H-13 – Small two-place helicopter made by Bell used for logistics on the icebreakers. Now retired.

HEC – High Endurance Cutters. During my time these were all Hamilton Class or 378" vessels.

IO – Ice operations.

Liberty Port – A geographical place where the crew is granted an opportunity to leave the vessel and go ashore for a period normally less than 24 hours. Approximately one quarter of the crew would have duty, which meant they had to stay aboard to maintain the ship's systems.

LE – Law Enforcement.

Lead Line – A handheld line with a weight on one end, marked off with depth at intervals normally fathoms, which are 6 feet in length. Used to determine the water depth for safe passage of a vessel.

Lightering – Removing the cargo from a vessel.

List – A nautical term meaning to tilt to one side.

Log - A logistics mission. An official journal of a ship's chronological history.

MDZ – Maritime Defense Zone

MEC – Medium Endurance Cutter. During my time these were primarily 210-foot vessels.

MEP – Marine Environmental Protection.

MSO – Marine Safety Office

MVS – Merchant Vessel Safety.

Nugget –Alaskan slang for a newcomer or greenhorn.

OSV – Ocean Station Vessel. A program of the Coast Guard in which Cutters were assigned safety station at the mid-way point of transoceanic flights. No longer operational.

Port – Left side of vessel, aircraft, of channel. Signified by a red light or a red buoy.

R – Readiness and Reserve Program. Originally handled military and contingency planning and managed the Service's small arms and ordnance programs. Also responsible for the military exercise program.

RCC – Rescue Coordination Center.

Roll – A nautical term meaning a vessel is rocking side to side caused by wave action.

RON – A mission that requires a crew to stay overnight at a location other than their home base.

RBS – Recreational Boating Safety.

SAR – Search and Rescue.

Starboard – right side of a vessel, aircraft, or channel signified by a green light at night or a green buoy.

Subsistence – A term indicating that a person or group of people survives by gathering natural food, animal or plant, from their environment.

VTS – Vessel Traffic System.

USLS – Lifesaving service.

Watching properly – A term meaning that a navigational aid is operating correctly.

Williwaw –Gusts of winds that can reach up to 110 MPH.

WPB – Coast Guard patrol boat.

WWII – World War Two.